Sh!t Men Say to Me

A Poetry Anthology
in Response to Toxic Masculinity

~ Edited by ~
Dania Ayah Alkhouli, HanaLena Fennel, & Victoria Lynne McCoy

MOON
TIDE PRESS

~ 2021 ~

Sh!t Men Say to Me: A Poetry Anthology in Response to Toxic Masculinity
© Copyright 2021 Moon Tide Press

Editor-in-chief
Eric Morago

Anthology Editors
Dania Ayah Alkhouli, HanaLena Fennel, & Victoria Lynne McCoy

Editor Emeritus
Michael Miller

Marketing Director
Dania Ayah Alkhouli

Marketing Assistant
Ellen Webre

Proofreader
Jim Hoggatt

Front cover art
Kat Keller

Interior art
Kia Hinton

Book design
Michael Wada

Moon Tide logo design
Abraham Gomez

Sh!t Men Say to Me: A Poetry Anthology in Response to Toxic Masculinity
is published by Moon Tide Press

Moon Tide Press
6709 Washington Ave. #9297
Whittier, CA 90608
www.moontidepress.com

FIRST EDITION

Printed in the United States of America

ISBN # 978-1-7350378-4-4

Contents

Foreword

While waiting for my order at a local Greek restaurant, a man passed by and suddenly changed his phone conversation. "These f***ing Muslims are taking over America, man!" I turned around to find him staring me down as he continued to walk away. The thing about toxic masculinity is that it does not just refer to sexist behaviors, but rather a whole spectrum of toxic reaction-driven tendencies. It also does not solely come from one gender, nor does it only affect one gender, but it stems from the stereotypical assumptions of how masculinity is to be presented.

Sometimes it feels like being a visibly Muslim Arab woman is defiance—and being an outspoken one at that is a revolution inviting toxic masculinity in like a moth to a flame. But to be fire is to be alive with passion and purpose, and I think of how often that is seen as such a threat to (toxic) masculinity, a call to be extinguished. It happens so frequently that sometimes we internalize expecting it. See, when Eric Morago, Editor-in-Chief of Moon Tide Press, first told me he wanted to publish my manuscript, I had a split second of confusion. A man was receiving my poetry, my fire, willingly? When so many of the poems I had written were in response to shit men had actually said to me? But it was his eagerness to highlight the brave voices with the fearlessness to speak up that convinced me Moon Tide Press is where my baby belongs, where these truths can further be solidified. And it was because of this publication, and a virtual poetry reading I did where I prefaced a poem of mine with its origins story, that the ideas began to flow.

What started out as a witty comment about how quite a few of my poems were about shit men say to me and how I could write a whole book on the topic, soon evolved into this incredibly necessary book you now hold before you. A collection of distinct voices intellectually braiding into poetry one common theme too many of us have grown exhausted by, shit men say to us. The greatest part of putting this book together was witnessing the diversity of poets offering their vulnerability, discussing the trauma, survival, and healing from toxic masculinity. From poems about coming of age to poems about an epiphany over coffee and cigarettes, this anthology powerfully illustrates the nuances of toxic masculinity with such impeccable and vivid imagery.

In a world that still tilts its hat to male privilege, it is our duty as editors and writers to carve out a space and share the narratives too often marginalized. There is no better place for this important platform than in Moon Tide Press's anthology, *Sh!t Men Say To Me*. I am unbelievably honored and humbled to have been an editor on this project alongside HanaLena Fennel & Victoria McCoy, and even more so I am immensely proud to be a part of such an inclusive family that allows and encourages everyone to authentically express themselves and bring to life both timeless and relevant collections worthy of finding a home on every shelf, including this one. I hope this book takes you on the same journey it took me when reading through the submissions—a journey of empathy, grief, courage, awareness, awakening, and love.

— Dania Ayah Alkhouli, 2021

Robin Axworthy

Landlocked 1971

The shark-teeth grind of the neighbor's chain saw
this morning hurled me back into winter snow,
knee deep drifts in new growth maple woods
populating the abandoned sheep farm hills.

You wielded the saw against the gray-ribbed arms
of fallen trees, I hauled out the long branches,
holding them steady while you cut them into cordwood
we stacked in the rusted bed of your old pickup.

My feet in too-tight winter boots grew cold,
then iced, then burned, then numb, but it was money
for food, gas, electricity to run the pump
from the well you'd had dug, our running water.

I wouldn't call it love. Back to the land, perhaps,
a kind of if-then longing which held me there
inside your wire fences, beating aside the grit
and constant grime, your appetites, your grand

theories of free sex, obedience porn, mushrooms
and self-sufficient poverty, so I could keep myself
in thrall, accept the hard-scrabble days, the cold nights,
glad for the wood stove holding coals safe overnight.

So, I could stay happy with our comedic ducks
and biddy-bossy hens, the warm hiss of milk
from our long-eared goat, while the dirt built up
in the wall-bed, between the cracks in the planked floor,

ground itself into our fingers and under our nails,
until I finally choked, raked all your words into a pile,
dead leaves, watched them smolder into ash—
an autumn chore, this getting rid of dead and gone.

KB Baltz

Loving Arms

I have fit
into the arms
of all my lovers
perfectly.
My head lays
just so on the crook
of their shoulder
when I rip
the voice
from my throat
leaving it bloody
on the floor
next to
hastily discarded cloths.

Devon Balwit

Poetess
After Sylvia Plath, "Lesbos"

And I, love, am a pathological liar.
I should wear tiger-pants, I should have an affair.
In New York, Hollywood, the men said: *Through?*
Gee baby, you are rare.

I fit my leg in a hollow stump, paint on wounds,
#MeToo, bead trauma like a patient in the day room.
And I, love, am a pathological liar.

This house, this street, are way too small.
Everyone knows me. They turn away.
I should wear tiger-pants, I should have an affair.

Screens drip phosphorous, phone-glow,
luminous blue. Selfies bellow like steer in a truck.
In New York, Hollywood, the men said: *Through?*
Gee baby, you are rare.

I cut myself, make myself vomit. See, see?
My eye shadow screams towards my hairline,
mouth a gash. And I, love, am a pathological liar.

I throw books against the wall, tear out pages.
Why them, why them? Do I not also prick my finger?
I should wear tiger-pants, I should have an affair.

Mentors rub against me like goats, waft
malodorous musk. They pour me glass after glass.
In New York, Hollywood, the men said: *Through?*
Gee baby, you are rare.

I lock my well-meaning parents in a small room.
No siblings, I lift some like butts from a can.
And I, love, am a pathological liar.

Such hungers the length of the Amazon
cannot satisfy. There must be a hex, a bargain.
I should wear tiger-pants, I should have an affair.

I pour over the Kama Sutra, tie myself in knots,
trace each night, purple from the lash.
In New York, Hollywood, the men said: *Through?*
Gee baby, you are rare. And I, love, am a pathological liar.

Amazonian

I didn't call you.
I didn't call you at all.

— *Sylvia Plath, "Medusa"*

What draws them to you—sight, smell
the clatter of your heels on cobbles,
the way your ass and titties bobble,
your forward lean, a boat through swell?
You feel them on your flank, the tell-
tale leer, the *Hey baby,* your *What the hell?*
choked back because who wants trouble?
You narrow your eyes and frown, double-
time it somewhere brighter, prepared to yell:
Off, off, eely tentacle! The spectacle
of a woman standing her ground,
hive sisters erupting murderous blades,
comes to mind and hovers, you an oracle
for some unborn generation of unbound,
armed, bare-breasted warrior maids.

What is marriage like?

my children ask, and I think
of the anglerfish, deep
in inky ocean, the female
groping her way with a torch
grown from her own body,
an iridescent lure for prey,
the male searching, searching, searching
perhaps his whole life long
without finding her, but if he does,
biting deep into her back or belly
and fusing until his organs
fade away, until he becomes little
more than a bulbous pair of testes
fringed with gills, protruding sack-like
as she plies her lantern.
[Therefore, shall he cleave
unto his partner, and the two
shall be one flesh] no immune response
one to the other, all that she has his
and vice versa until death.
Such teeth, my children,
you have never seen
such teeth.

Eryn Berg

Guardrails

My own son, stopped short of his 9th grade year, complains about missing friends
but sits closer to me on the couch than puberty usually allows.

He is the same age I was when Paul died—
My first bona fide death if you don't count grandfathers I barely knew.

I felt stuck those years, inside the brokenness Highway 26 felt like freedom,
and I let his friend kiss me and wore his leather jacket that smelled like cigarette
smoke
and was banished to our garage.

He was not the boy my Mom should have been afraid of.

The hallways were full of rumors of death that morning, the school year new.
He was short and funny and inside the shattered glass of imagined car wrecks,
he stayed young forever.

There was a moment of silence but inside dirty bathrooms we avoided
loudspeakers and rolled around on cold floors.
His safety pins dug into my skin and I had only myself to blame.

My parents said Jesus, but I could only see guardrails, and we drank ourselves
away from boys who die.

Later there were others.
The boy who fell off a mountain.
The shotgun in the mouth.
The suicides that took thirty years.

I tried to shake the stalking sadness.
For years I outran it until finally it confronted me in a bathroom
mirror, and I cracked into fragments.

I collected all those broken pieces, and at the corners of the darkness
I saw flickers of light.

And I tell my son that on the other side of this windshield is blue sky.
I squeeze his hand and whisper to myself, *please please please please—*

never go.

Elya Braden

Words in My Mouth

My husband begs me to play Scrabble,
a game I only play with girlfriends
or strangers in online chatrooms.
Memories of doubles tennis together
as newlyweds still sting. Tonight,
I've run out of ways to say: *NO*.
I shake the tiles in the bag, speak only
the letters I am given. He hoards
his feckless "V" and clumsy "Q,"
dreaming of seven-letter bingos
until I add *XI* to morph the "E"
he dangled over a triple letter
square into *EX*. A premonition?
50 points for a triple-triple!
How dare you? he roars.
That space was mine!
I reach into the box and dredge up
all the wooden squares
my small hands can hold,
tiles slipping through my fingers,
lost opportunities for *HOPE*
or *FREEDOM, JOY* or *KINDNESS.*
I open my mouth. I'm a Baleen whale
inhaling the sea. I stuff tiles
into my wide red hole, gulping
his "B" (3 points) for *BITCH,*
"WH" (oh, that winning combination
of 4 and 4) for *WHORE,*
"S" (only 1 point) but handy
for *SHOUT* and *SHIT, SELFISH*
and *SATISFY*, a bingo he won't get tonight.
I swallow the "U" from the *SLUT*
he thinks I am to isolate his solitary "Q,"
along with all the "I's" from his:
YOU IDIOT and my: *I'M SORRY*
to block his *QI.* "L's" drip from

my lips for all the *LOVE YOU'S*
I've used to placate him. My tongue
savors the sensuous grooves
of the "O" for all the *ORGASMS*
he hasn't given me and for *OVER*,
the cliff we are about to plunge.

What to Think Of
after Mark Strand

Think of the palm trees whispering
danger, danger to the wind

the tropical moths bigger than your
small hand whooshing in and out

empty rectangles cut in walls
windows in a colder climate.

Think of the waves rising up
to celebrate the night, clapping

their froth-fringed fingers
on the rocky shore

the sand that singed your toes
now cool with darkness.

Think of the white sheets kneading
your back as you writhe

under the inescapable weight of his
thick body, his knees pinning

the butterfly of you to this mattress.
Think of the steel-wool forest rioting

from his barrel chest. Do not glance
at his face turbulent with drink.

Do not smell his breath, rotten
with cigarillos and scotch.

Do not scream as he twists
your nipples to red pain.

Do not cringe when he caresses the curve
of your jaw, growls: *I'll hit you here.*

Think of the sand, the seagrass,
the long trek to the nearest bungalow

the dark buzzing with bats and beetles.
Think of your phone, your passport

your wallet all locked in a safe
to which he holds the key.

Think of the silk scarves he knotted
into blindfolds and hand ties

in the distant comfort of your apartment
that night you went short-skirt *commando*

at an oceanfront bistro, his twiddling
cloaked under white tablecloth

as you giggled, flirted with the flame-
haired waitress

and know: no one would believe
you didn't ask for this.

How to Be Deposed

Apply two coats of waterproof mascara.
Floss until it steadies your hands. Sit down
while you sheath your winter legs
in ultra-sheer pantyhose, Nude #2. Remember
the time before your ninth deposition,
teetering in your hallway in a twisted
tree pose, you wrenched your back,
flailing like a netted trout.
Do not bat your eyelashes at your lover,
I mean, lawyer, until you two are alone
in a taxi fleeing the scene.
Don't shriek when plaintiff's counsel
accuses you of sleeping with
the defendant. Try to forget
that co-counsel's son carpools
with your daughter. Count the lines
in the wood grain of the
conference room table. Hum
in your head to the rat-a-tat
of the stenographer's flying fingers.
Breathe. Wait for your lawyer's objection.
Later, when he asks: *Was it true?*
don't slap him. Don't place a straight razor
near your bubble bath. Leave
your pearl-handled revolver at home,
tucked under your monogramed hankies.
Remember you don't have a revolver…
or hankies. Remember all the dimes
you earned ironing your father's hankies.
Try to forget his shadow in your doorway.
Try to forget his hand over your mouth.
Try to forget the sticky touch of your brother's
beanbag chair on your bare thighs,
your brother's threat: *I'll tell everyone what you did.*
Try to forget his needling question:
Does it feel good when I touch you here?

Eric Braman

Toothbrush

we catch eyes
in my reflection
the face of
someone I don't
know
moss and allspice
peppercorn and iron
cedar and sulfur
he left
in my mouth his
taste
I brush my teeth
to get the grime
of ghosts off
my gums
each bristle
   those words
I was raised to
understand
    suck my dick
as a threat
I don't recognize
these eyes
like driving through
cattails to reach
seawalls and sandbars
filled with grains of
    faggot
    pansie
    fairy
they pile up until
waters recede
and all I'm left
with behind my lips is
plaque built-up
on yellowed teeth

cavities from chewing on
    fruitcake
and
    sod
you taste like
Miller Lite
I could never stand
your stale flavor
but I chipped my
teeth chewing the
tough leather it
takes to
    be a man
I brush with
artificial mint
trying to cover
the flavor of
fir needles and
autumn leaves
I'm not the man
my reflection
thought I would be
I brush
and brush
and brush
until I bleed
iron and rust
    man up
lava rock and gasoline
    man up
you tell me
you thought I was stronger
as I scrape the roots
expose my nerves
I brush until
I have no teeth left
I brush so hard
the words fall out
one at a time
bloodstains swirling
down the drain

and my reflection
wonders
how to
swallow
the truth with
no teeth

Christina Brown

September

I am learning to endure the loneliness of your daylight.
To hold out for the whiskey evenings
when you call to say you miss me
and you're sorry
and can't we just be us again, tonight.
I am learning to love myself,
but only in the dark.
I am learning to make a feast
of the crumbs you offer.
To stop expecting a forever
that lasts longer than you want it to.

I am learning to measure reality in half-lives
the way scientists measure radioactive decay.
I am learning to say
This is how long I can hold this truth
between my fingers while it shrinks.
I am learning to shrink with it.
My grips slips with every introduction
of a new half-truth,
of someone else's revision or memory.
I am always slamming my fists together
a story squeezed in each hand
trying to make myself whole again
with all your broken parts.

Sure Is a Scary Time for Boys

I too would like to pay my rent by quiet drum pulse.
Would like my echo to be heard & named.
Would like to call a body mine.
I too would like a loud and unchoked pipeline voice
microphone.
I too would like a man to scream in prayer before I can spill.
To call me worthy of survival in the wake of his violence.
I too would like an army.
I too would like to be of value even boneless.
I too wish to be impermeable
thick.
I wish to be not the gems encrusted
but the whole hard crown
wrapped around the ruler
tighter and tighter.

Show Me Your Wings

My father rode his motorcycle home
on the only day we had butterflies this year.
He came home covered in yellow gold slaughter.
He told me LA had never been so beautiful
and full of wings.

When I was young
my grandparents had a cabin in the mountains
up a windy road that always made me sick.
My grandfather set off moth bombs
in the empty house every year
but some always survived.
Brown gray and wispy and gnawing
our clothes in the closets
though my mother promised they didn't bite.

I can't help but wonder if I know what it means
to be cut from the ugly side of the cloth,
or if it matters to be called beautiful
if they will kill you anyway.

Tony Brown

Men I Know

A man I know
calls his preferred
prospective partners
"chicklettes."
Because they're young,
young and sweet,
he says.
Because of their fragile shells,
he says.
Because he spits them out
when the flavor's gone,
he says.

This other man I know
has jokes up the wazoo
about women, about
"how they are."
Because that's just
letting off steam,
he says.
Because of the need for a break
in the battle between us,
he says.
Because it's better than shooting them,
he says,
and laughs.

This other man I know
likes to stick his elbow into me
whenever he pretends he's down
for women where we work.
Because they think I mean it,
he says.
Because as men we know the score,
he says.
Because, anyway, where were we before they talked?
he says.

Other men I know lose track
of bedmate headcount.
Other men keep track,
notch something to brag about.

Other men I know have heard about "no,"
but they say it's just a lock to be picked apart.
Other men don't care much for locks,
bust down the door, swear they heard a cry
for help in there.

I know many other men who I'd have sworn
are none of these,
but too often I learn of one or more who are
not the men I thought they were
and now when I say

this other man I know
or
these other men I know.

I stop and wonder
if other men are in fact knowable,
why I seem to know so many of these other men,
and why those other men
seem so comfortable with me.

Cathleen Calbert

Flower-Eating Season

It's spring, and my dazed dog
      devours all flowers, our walks
          punctuated by munches. She's more
     than happy, gulping down small blue flutes
and decapitating dandelions.
       Looking at my flower-glutton of a mutt,
          I think of cunnilingus, what a struggle
   for some men to get down on their knees,
that boy a thousand years ago
     who said *Oh, I like it*
        because you like it,
     which made me never want him
to push his face between my legs again.
       My husband used to assiduously
          put his mouth upon my flower
     when we were young(ish) and green(ery)
until I newly bloomed, shall we say.
     What's taking her so long?
          asked the fellow watching
a "sex awareness" film as a woman
on screen swam twenty minutes
      towards the shore of her orgasm,
         those slow sweet strokes far
    from porn or whores or this old guy,
friend of the family, whose "supported"
     consort, one third his age, comes,
         he claims, twice in five minutes.
    No, she doesn't, I want to say.
Are you an idiot? I want to say
     to my husband. *It's flower-eating season.*
        What lies before us but age and death?
    Remember how we slept
in the same big bed and you weren't
     too fatigued to please me? Instead
         I walk my crazy girl, who wants to
    swallow the world, and I've bought myself

a vaseful of flowers: red roses surrounded
by irises and lilies as wild as pink leopards.
Well, there's always my own hand
and still my guy's kind smile. I'm faithful,
or at least not unfaithful, as Larkin
might have said, though I must confess
nowadays I turn more to cummings.

I Don't Want to Read a Poem About Baseball

I'm tired of the American spirit,
the boys of summer and their fans,
team effort and hey batta batta.

Maybe it's just another thing
that I don't understand.
Like God or jogging.

But I was that black-clad chick
behind the bleachers, smoking.
I don't know anything

about sports, period.
(My brother shakes his head:
"There are many ways to be stupid.")

True, for me there was no beauty,
no satisfying crack of ball and bat,
just another chance to be a girl

without hand-eye coordination.
A ball coming in my direction
meant I should do three things:

duck, cross
my arms like an X
over my head, and wait for death.

I've got enough
adult humiliations
to write about already, don't you?

Shouldn't your poems be
about girls like me anyway?
How you loved kissing us in the rain?

How nothing was better
than the mist of menthol
between our shining lips?

Don't get me wrong.
I don't care if you play the game.
Have fun. Slide into home.

But I don't want to
bask in the amber glow
of another boyhood in Brooklyn,

hear about your World Series
heartbreak or existential loneliness
first encountered in the outfield.

Don't try to prove
you're not as fey as a poet
by applauding jocks, please.

I don't want to read those poems
just like you don't want to
read about my body.

Since you're the editors,
you win, you rock, you rule.
The rest of us are pussies.

Michael Cantin

Does the Abyss Stare Back?

I see you stare empty eyed—
a madman working soundless lips
while you focus at your study.

What wonders might you find
clamoring towards the light
in those dark recesses?

What ancient and terrible truths
could there possibly be
lurking unseen

within her Cleavage?

Jan Chronister

What It's Like

It's that smell I can't get rid of—
dead-mouse odor even though
I've washed the fabric over and
over, hung it in sun. It's when I run
out of thread on all my
spools, those from my
mother, those I hang on to
so I don't lose my way. It's the
dread that I will run into
you or just think your name.
It's the hope that you are dead.
When you are finally gone
I will find that lost piece of
my past, flush you down the toilet
one last time.

C. Cropani

Cousin

My cousin
not the one on my dad's side
came into my bedroom
one fine Thanksgiving
shut the door,
locked it.

I was wearing my favorite
red and white dress
with the giant bow
and bigger than my head
stationed at the neck.

And this cousin—
The one assigned to say
grace up to God
for this year's feast—
sat on my bed
and said,

Close your legs.
You're attracting flies.

I pushed him off the bed
unlocked the door, bolted
out the back, ran
down the hill, scaled
up my tree fort
sobbing, spreading
my legs, looking
for flies. They
never came.

When Thanksgiving was over
and all the cars were gone
I returned to my house, trashed
my clothes, and cursed all things
cousins.

Later
when my sister
and I were older
staring down the casket
of my cold, stiff cousin
I told her what he said
and how it landed
me in the fort, and
my dress in the trash, with
a hatred for Thanksgiving
an aversion to cousins
a disdain for my legs
and everything in between
an obsession with flies, and
years of psychotherapy,
she said,

Fucking Capricorn.
Only a Capricorn
could take down
an entire childhood
in one
shot.

Alexis Rhone Fancher

Domestic Violence

Knives cut both bread and throats, he warns, the stiletto's steel tip teasing my trachea. A love tap. I'm used to it. I don't react anymore; I bake. I knead, pound the dough instead of him. Each day when he leaves for court, those $2,000 suits camouflaging his viciousness, a brief reprieve. I envision his face in the smacked-down dough, push out the air pockets, dream of suffocation. I slap him, punch him, only to watch him rise. While he proofs, I look for loopholes, binge-watch *Forensic Files*, its endless stories of stymied desire, hour after hour of scheme and kill, each murder more gruesome, honed. I take notes, stick in a shiv to see if he's done, plot that he comes to a similar bad end. I shape loaves like alibis, knife-notched before they go into the oven, frenzied jabs and slices. I sharpen the blade, ready for his return. Like him, I'll never speak without a lawyer present.

After the Restraining Order Expires, M. Begs Me to Meet Him for Lunch

Says he 'killed it' in anger management class,
that everything's under control. Bygones.

I drink my unrequited malice.
Wonder how soon he'll turn deadly.

You're a sip, he says, *barely a swallow.*
He laps up my resistance,

leans over, nuzzles my neck,
wraps his arm around my indecision.

Remind me again why we broke up?
He was always a fine interrogator.

I watch his shirt ride up above his belly,
where I'd lay my head to suck him off.

The desperation of his stark, white skin,
the crude exposure.

I'd pull his shirt back down,
but it would be too much like tenderness.

Freeway Sex

There's a 19-car pile-up on Vasquez Rocks.
You're late. This would be a good excuse.

I want to grind that thought out like your cigarette.
Drive right over it.

You were dead to me the first time
I found motel matches
in your pocket.

You brought me offramp roses.
Your fingers smelled like someone else.

When the traffic doesn't move
when I'm lost again in Pasadena
and my pussy dampens,
I think of fellating you on the freeway
to pass the time.

Is that what you're thinking of?

From the 5 to the 2 to the 134.
Take the Pearblossom Highway.
Make a smooth transition.

Tell me exactly how it's going down and
I'll write that poem.

The one where you're supposed to
be on time, and I'm supposed to care.

Stina French

Mirror, Mirror

I made the mistake once of telling Bobby Cress that the weirdest thing I'd ever used to masturbate was a Snicker's bar, still in the wrapper. He used to walk up to me for years after that and say, "it really satisfies" to remind me he knew my dirty little secret.

I guess I thought that chocolate seemed the best answer out of all the other weird shit I stuffed up my cunt and asshole. What else did I use? Hairbrush handle. Knife handle. Pencil. Electric toothbrush. Aunt Evelyn's spa tub jets. My favorite: the squiggle wiggle writer.

I will get my daughter a vibrator when she's ready, a real one, but I see nothing wrong with these creative acts of insertion and insurrection. Women get pushed right out of our bodies and minds so often, no wonder we spend so much time trying to get back in.

The thing I used most often was a hard, travel-size can of Barbasol. It had a divot in the bottom, the end I inserted lest the cap come loose inside me. And like a tiny mountaintop lake, it filled with the sticky ivory jelly of my curious girl cunt. I can still see the white, navy blue, and maroon stripes on the upright, respectable masculine container. Sometimes, before I washed off the can and put it back into my step-father's medicine cabinet, I'd stare at the perfect little pool, stick a finger into it, taste it.

I can still see the tableau of ex-Army man medicine cabinet. Electric razor, straight razor, disposables, too. Irish Spring soap in the box. Shower cleaner spray that mom made him keep there. One or two of her bobby pins he used to clean out his ears. And extra-large nail clippers.

I used to have to trim his toenails. He said it was because he couldn't reach them anymore. The big toe's nail was split down the middle, leaving a sickening strip of scar tissue, a valley surrounded by jutting rock formations of yellow fungus-infected nail. Me an 8-year old girl, holding those extra-large clippers meant for exactly this kind of gross too-thick old man toenail. Each click brought a sickening rush to my gut. I always seemed to get hit in the eye by this or that stray piece of shrapnel. You know what's grosser? That I was so fucking desperate for connection I didn't mind. I looked forward to this little service ritual. It was about the only time I felt needed. The only time I felt I'd done something right.

Let me be a little more honest with you. I didn't always clean off the little can of Barbasol when I was done with it. I can still see my face in the mirror above his sink when I went to fetch my inanimate partner in sin. The same mirror I stared into repeating the mantra I learned from all the boys at school. "You are so ugly. You are so ugly. You are so ugly." Downstairs, mother stared into her own mirror, a looking glass that magnified her flaws and stray chin hairs. I came a long way to get here. Into this body. Don't think because I told you all the shit I used to put inside me that you're in there now, too.

She Cracks the Door

You spend years 11 to 17 staring nightly at a crack of light formed by your bedroom door standing slightly ajar. Rehearsing your planned reaction. Your sister gives you this room, her room, when you turn 11, when you hit puberty, when she leaves. She says to you, she says, "lock the door at night, Christy." But you don't. This crack of light opens the plot of family, beyond what we should reasonably expect to happen inside family, but it does not offer a way out. Sometimes, you eat each other in there.

Your position in relation to the crack of light is a restrictive clause. Unpausing. Wanting proof, you dangle, willing bait in the dark. You want to know what's coming for you. You want to watch his silhouette grow large in your vision until you can be sure. If he comes for you, you'll kill him. What big teeth you cut then, holding knives under pillows in the dark. You stare at the crack in the door. You lose the fuller picture. You see in pinpoint. Line of sight. Your vision unmoors itself from you, you disappear and are all arrow, all arch. You stare at that crack and become your own erasure. The only way out is through. You leave your body, but your eyes stay open. You stare until you are all slit. Gaping. All of you, a response to a threat. You want to become the bigger threat.

Remember the strip of cowhide hanging below his big old-man belly? Remember him saying, "You got a tool this big, you gotta build a shed over it." Remember him unbuckling, sliding it off through worn loops. He folds the leather. Grinning. Gripping the ends, he makes it pucker. Pulls fast. Space collapses. He makes it snap. Hear that? Hear that? He wants to make a hole where the girl was. Each crack of his belt startles you from yourself. When you get mouthy, when you act smart.

They say shame can't survive in the light. If enough light gets through, maybe you can all be saved. But what if no light gets through because the child's body is filling the crack? The child's mind fills the crack and leaves her body. Her widening eyes in the dark. Awaiting penetration by shadow. A silhouette of all belts off.

Look how well he silenced your sister. She tells you, be quiet, too. Says it isn't yours to tell. If his shadow had solidified, become substance from nightly scare, would you have the right to name him? If it had been worse, it would have been your story then? Are you ready for what happens when you tell it? This is the way the girl ends. This is the way the girl ends. She won't love you anymore.

Cecilia M. Gigliotti

The Helen Shoot

Be still, they said,
this face is gonna launch a thousand ships.
I didn't ask where they'd be launched.
I did as I was told:
let them slash off my hair
and dull my sightline to a dead end;
lay on the floor,
propped up on smooth elbows,
neck craned back,
legs against the wall;
slouched in a doorway,
lids heavy,
lips just parted.
A million-millimeter lens
to grant me grace,
always the shutter
snapping in my face.
A band of executives with cigar-smoke haloes,
a detail of stylists wearing one demonic grin.
Let's see that bitch Atalanta top this.

Stephanie Gigliozzi

Stiletto in Gloss

Your sweaty grip
guarded me like silver
chain link fences

Your moustache,
tickling the back of my neck
tells the world I am spoken for

You saw the way married drummers watched me
through dressing rooms
You had to keep me close
I was a backstage peep
that could ruin the lives of men

You wanted me
you loved how I paint the town and the sky
in anzerat and hummingberry
Colours that pierced
the white sheets in your eyes

I could pull thigh-high boots up just enough
for you to reach realms of purple moons,
where wet drops fell from my chest
glossing the night's long lips

Vanilla tobacco / jealousy
oozed from your neck pores
whenever I spoke to *any other*
You could smell the ones
that wanted to fuck

Temptress
written red on my forehead
Lust harbour bruised purple on my forearms
Sweetness burst orange down my legs
You thought these were my only colours,
and missed the canvas of love

You sat there, in a pink cloud outside my window
for too long
The crowds below all hummed
Jackson, Mississippi blues for me
Bluer rose-petal swirls of loneliness

I kept telling you it wouldn't work,
I lived here and you there—
No matter what I said, you'd always come back
You loved the way I fit

I got off on the rock God under my thumb
masturbating with picks and razor blades, 'till I came
and let the demons in
and the walls that follow me
to every lover's door

Later, you wanted closure
asking if there was ever love—
maybe

But my talent, my talented dear
there are so many paintings in the sky,
how can I possibly close my eyes
to all that waiting colour?

Kristen Grace

Love Letter for Holly and Sex Without Power

I was watching a bee make love to a hollyhock,
then another and another,
without damaging a single petal.

The bee got so exhausted,
so covered in pollen, she fell asleep
inside her lover.

I was reminded of my Holly, my first kiss—
of all our kisses—and my sweet, secret introduction to sex.
Together, we were safe from any kind of power struggle
or from the toxic idea of sin.

We would curl up inside our turned-out sleeping bags,
protected and warm in one another's arms,
buried in our long hair, and discover bliss.

When we finally fell asleep in a field of cartoon candy pink,
we would jointly dream of better futures and kinder partners
than we would be blessed to find for decades.

Anne Graue

Eve's World, Clear as Water

She spoke to the one not yet close enough to the ground
but close to desire, the flesh, sour and sweet. It must have been,

for her to convince, to suggest, to offer a taste, or out of malice,
perhaps—so that she wouldn't be alone in her knowledge, so that

he might know it too—to push it into his hand. Had she known,
seen the signposts in the murk, she might have faltered, but her vision

had cleared, shapes appeared in outline, cartoonish after
the nightmare. She blinked to see better through the watery dark, heard

a voice rising through radio noise, saw trees bent, yellow, and sharp.

Michael Gravagno

Hit Hit

        And then I hit you
but it's not like I—not hit
        you hit you.
It was an accident, I slipped

                        just like men
always say they slipped,
              and then it hit me
    what if I'm
           that I am

just like them.

        They. What if
                      they're just like me?
    But
                I always hated
those kinds of brutish, violent me—

        Not how it happened, we
were both drunk and walking and
           you just kept whittling

        and I stewed in boozy silence

and then you hit me play

    -fully. Thought I should snap
                  back
    a bit,   but

                but it was harder
than I meant, my fist
        hit an organ,

your kidney it was
                    an accident

and we stopped
        walking and our friend, he
                    said "I wish I hadn't
                                seen that," not "I wish
                        that hadn't happened,"
and he walked away

        fast as you cried and I

                                            puddled
in belief that this is in me
        now—this

                    potential me,

        this
violence,

me,   these men,   me.

    And I didn't think
then, because I was saying
"I'm sorry,   I'm so so sorry,   I didn't
mean to—

        But now I think that men who
hit
        must slip   once
and then it hits them

        what's been there all
along—out slipped that potential, them,

that   violence,

            them,   me
and then

they   keep   hitting
        until   they keep hitting until
                          they keep hitting

                until it doesn't

                                hit them anymore.

Kelly Gray

One in Three

I often wonder at the Language of Statistics,
The Bureau of Boyhood,
The Land Management of Men,
the memberships due.

I imagine if I had the audacity of a cock
to break into this meeting, this alliance,
my teeth as sharp as my knife,
throat bound, on bull horn,
to ask them, who of you are the rapists?

Some men will hear this question
and take to the windows,
shattering glass and expectation
from suit to asphalt flat.

Some men will run off, mouths gagged,
leaving lovers and suitcases behind,
splayed out across highways
to take their chances with truckers and coyotes and rest stops.

Some men will resort to violence,
cutting off their daughter's ears
so that she will never hear the sound of another man she loves telling her
This is how you show me you love me.

Some men will take to the kitchen
to pour burning coffee across hands,
searing the prints from her legs,
soft thigh hair from their fingers.

Some men will become seamstresses,
sewing mouths and legs shut,
thread made of threat.

Some men will lie,
twisting tangent and tail,
eating lamb with bent forks.

Worse though, one may tell truth.

Then,
I will be required to love a man
who has muffled a voice,
required to kiss a clavicle where
it has rubbed up against a face,
smashed.

We are all broken birds,
bent,
our song beneath the tires
as they flee
from offices of their design,

and I do not have the audacity of a cock,
to call out after them,
who of you, who of you have done this?

Caroline Hedel

In Which I Rearticulate Myself Among the Living

I am presently as compelled to write as I am
to wash myself incessantly and cat-like
meaning rough
and by rough meaning that's how you like it that's how you like it
your preference is food off the floor
and foot soles clean
and elbow creases white and shiny;
someone said I would have been
neurotic in the old days,
which makes me laugh because now I am
a side character
in an agatha christie novel
in the manor, or on the beach
she who saw the murderer face-to-face just before fainting
and after that page was never heard from again.
relax, said every man I ever knew, to me
if you don't tense up it won't hurt
and you might even like it,
you might even live to see the end of the novel
if the author doesn't first forget that you
were ever written into existence.

Tanya Ko Hong

The War Still Within

Tonight my tongue cuts galaxy
black bones be fire
a crying cello drifting
if I open my mouth
I will be sent to the Taklimakan
Desert a graveyard
silence of a thousand skulls
Endless black
Nothing can live
My eyes a flame
I never talk about the battleground
My secret burns there
My silence is your mouth
My skull the house of story
My jaw hinges
star-dirt
devastation in a capsule

White man said
> *No one listens to you*
> *No one sees*
> *Open your mouth*

I said
> *Go ahead*
> *Cut and burn my tongue*
> *You can't set fire my secrets*
> *My other tongue*
> *will speak*
>
> *I carry my eyes, my bones*
> *through this war*

Jonathan Humanoid

The Shape of Masculinity

I haven't weighed myself in a year.
The last time I weighed in I was one hundred and sixty-eight point nine.
That was two years ago;
three antidepressants/and their weight gain ago/one identity revolving
around my body and
an I-thought-I-was-in-love ago.

I am standing in front of a mirror. Partially dressed. Brushing my teeth.
It is not my place. These are not my toothbrush or toothpaste. My
reflection stares back at me. The glass is etched with 168.9—nearby
I can hear water running/sex and a shower/a natural order. The
apartment is hers. I watch her walk up behind me/touch my waist/tell
me I am better shape than the last two men to stand in my spot.

Beneath my feet the carpet feels new.
I am the first to flex my toes here.
Her admiration carves lines into my face.
When I look back to myself/
I see my worth etched into my skin.
168.9

She says she likes me
for my intelligence.
This is the semester she is both my lover
and professor.
We are adults/so it feels fine.

She likes me/we are dating/so it feels fine.
I am sometimes slow/as a student.
I have a lot to learn.
I won't realize how wrong I am
about all of those thoughts/until the second
or the third time/that she has mentioned my muscles.

And I want to say we still talked. About books.
And not how I could be doing better as a student.

But god/ how I could feel fresh carpet/new home/ place to become love
whenever she noticed the tension/ of my arms/ or my back/ or my stomach.

The last time we talked/ she asked if I had written any angry poems about
her. I have written poems. I don't think they were angry. Not at her. I have
been congratulated for bedding a fantasy. Weird as that feels to me. The
poems are not about that, definitely. I want to say they are poems of pain. I
hurt for a long time. Weight gain felt like failure.

I broke up with her/ my mirror broke up with me. Both relationships
ended messily.

This poem is also not angry. I recently weighed two hundred and six point
3 pounds. I am thicker than a luchador. My reflection and I are cool again. I
am talking to a woman who listens when I talk. Sighs and swoons a bit when
I read poems even if they are not about her. Inhales deeply when I share a
thought that has excited me and I feel smart. I think it's kind of funny. The
shape of masculinity I am discovering is not fluid. It is brick. It is mortar.
This poem is a chisel. To chip at my insecurities. To chip at the success of sex.
To carve of myself something more. Not to make of myself art. But to free
what has been trapped in this rigid stone for this entire time. ~~168.9~~ Value.

LeAnne Hunt

Mathematics for Lady Poets and Girl Lab Techs: Word Problems for Women

Let me tell you about my trouble with girls...three things happen when they are in the lab... You fall in love with them, they fall in love with you and when you criticize them, they cry.

— Nobel Laureate Tim Hunt

VIDA counts. I am making bank—
female cents to male dollars,
publication creds. and post doc studies,
women's names are not seen nor heard.

If approximately 50% of the US population
is female
and more than 60% of English and
communication majors
are female
but 70% of authors *The Atlantic*
published or reviewed in 2016
were male,
find the missing women.
Solve for drowning.

Statistics are hard
for the soft spoken,
worse for the strident labeled.
Lily Ledbetter gives good
alliteration, but a woman
is designed for assonance
and bearing.

Women wear diamonds, but men wear
women on their arms. Study finds
that men sparkle with 'inherent brilliance'
in the poppy fields of math, physics, philosophy
and music composition. Women's talents

are not raw enough for tenure. Weigh
hard work against innate talent,
subtract for empathy. Round by
using Salic law.

If woman, W, performs same job
equally as man, M, but is paid 6% less
and W has a child, with wage penalty
of 4% per child
and M has the fatherhood bump of 6%,
solve for decreased access
to birth control.

Head versus heart,
remember, cupcake, your talent
lies in laying down
before biological laws.
You need to bleed.
Weigh the gray matter.
Planetary origins, Venus or Mars.
Pluto was demoted for skirting the issue.
Show a little—not too much—
cleavage, legs, ankles, skin.
The ruler boasts six inches of
solid wood.

Total the area
of the triangle kitchen design.
Calculate the steps taken
between refrigerator, sink and stove
to the nearest choice
reduced by expectation.
Find Bermuda.

Vicki Iorio

The Test

When he choked me, I did not see
red flags but pinpricks of light. Right
before I passed out, he released

his hand. We were in his mother's
bay house, she was a queen sleeping in the king-size,
he told me strangulation was a test.

His mother, upon surfacing kissed me
with lips tasting like bitter apples,
made up my bed with curling rose petals.

The blizzard dimmed the lights—
snow fell like a climax in a fairy tale,
doors froze and the bay locked. Fish

took their cold hearts far below,
swans linked necks on the shoreline.
When I escaped to the ice

a test of my toe made the surface snap
like a hyoid bone.

Sushi '81

There is a sailor with a hostess in the tatami room. They close
the curtains, we hear humping while we sip our miso soup.
It is Pearl Harbor Day—40 years later.

My husband is the greatest guy, everyone thinks so. The
sushi chef calls him Gary-san. Gary is a lover not
a fighter. The licensed chef is a samurai of fish.

He prepares fugu, extracts the liver and the
ovaries, the source of tetrodotoxin. Gary jokes
about being a survivor of my PMS. There is no

antidote for this poison, paralysis and silence—
the way Gary likes me. The chef has a special
treat for my Gary. Like a porno fluffer, the danger of eating

puffer makes Gary hard. The sushi bar patrons cheer
Gary on. I am hoping for treachery. I am rooting for the
Japanese.

Victoria Irwin

While I Tried to Write

While I tried to write this,
He interrupted to tell me his elbow hurt,
And asked what we were having for lunch.

As I debated sentences,
He told me about a misplaced delivery,
And turned on the television.

While I questioned word choices,
He asked me again what I was doing,
So, this poem is short.

Ryan Johnson

Detour

Dad is driving 40 in a 25
as if he wants to be home
and muttering about Mom
as if he doesn't.
Then the car lurches to a crawl,
straddles the bike lane,
and the low wolf-whistle
of a practiced predator
tells me there's something
a 14-year-old should notice,
other than his horny dad
enveloping him in booze-mist.
Now that's a rack,
he says to no one willing to hear,
I'd grab her and bring her home,
he shrivels me to the void,
Or do you think she's more your age?
And at this explicit nod
that he is giving his son the wereman's bite,
that he thinks this is a cultural practice
not only worth keeping for himself
but necessary to pass down,
I sit on the curb of my adolescence
and it takes me 15 years
before I can believe a woman
        would say *yes* to a man
        when men are like this.

Nikoline Kaiser

Stop the Traffic

This is a place
we've been before
And I've told you
stop the traffic
I'm bleeding out here

The train hit her
ninety-seven kilometers
per hour
Not the fastest train
you inform her
as she lies bleeding
It truly is a miracle,
that you are still alive

This place, we've been here before
stop the traffic
there's a woman on the tracks, she's bleeding
The tracks are red, crimson, you say
it's a much prettier word
you say
Would you like to know,
the etymology
of the word
crimson
There's a woman
bleeding on the tracks,
I say
you say,
It's a word from
old Spanish

(it's Arabic if we go back even further
I don't tell him that
there's a woman bleeding on the tracks)

We've been here before
this bar with sticky surfaces
sticky hands
a train
I am being told
can go so fast, did you know
350 km per hour
for the fastest
of trains

There's not enough vodka in the bar
to make this conversation interesting
I've been raised polite though
so, I smile
and I listen
and I remember, walking home
that a train can go
three-hundred and fifty kilometers
per hour
He was probably just nervous
so, he ran his mouth
three hundred and fifty-one
kilometers
per minute

The train hit her
not the fastest train
(I've been informed)
stop the traffic
I say
there's a woman bleeding out here
I'm the woman bleeding out here
and he says
Actually
you can't stop the traffic
it is always in motion
you can halt it
for a time
but you cannot stop it, can you, truly
I didn't know they sent
fucking philosophers
with their ambulances
now

This is a place,
we've been before
and I am telling you
that I am bleeding
and she is bleeding
Oh, but why,
the three hundred and ninety-seven onlookers
who have gathered,
ask
why
would she step in front of that train?
The leading cause of suicide in women
is depression
he informs me

I don't know
I think maybe
you were telling her
about the etymology of the word crimson
and she saw how fast the train was going
and thought
that'll do

The blood on the tracks
Is closer to burgundy
I'd say

L. Kardon

For Richard

There's one editor
I've sent work to
who always says
the poems make a nice
music. Sometimes

he calls them innocent, if
they're not gruesome
enough (he'll need me
to spell out the trauma,
really earn it)

or if they are, he'll say
they're cloaked and angry,
heavy with an inexplicable
rage toward the world.

Inexplicable? Shit,
Richard I'm raising
a child alone in a
world where the doctors
run a finger 'round
your rim without so
much as asking.

The best part is when
he compares my work to
Plath's, as though he'd
never read the work
of another poet-assigned-female
before (or since,
and maybe he hasn't).

I think to myself,
Jesus, of course
you're the type
to romanticize

the writer who stuck
her head in the oven,
as her babies slept.

The Mailman

You were loathsome
in the morning.
With all your night's terrors
stashed in the pocket at your breast.
I think you might have cooked
your own blood if you'd
thought it would get you high.

And all the while I'm dousing
the plants with bloody water—
they're nigh enough to carnivores
in the lonesome woman's house.

In the morning, when you roiled
through the house, shaking
the cabinets and dislodging bits of
foundation, the mailman
would make himself ever so quiet—
tiptoeing past, barely touching the
box.

Hamburgers

When I first left my ex
for the last time
(on and off
for 12 years with never
a true remission)
when I first left him
that time, our baby
was not yet two.

He was an angry man
(surely still is—you can't
fix that kind of rage).
He'd get red-faced, throw
things, break his own shit
(TV, plates, clothing rack—
whatever). He was
moody. A quick victim.

Once he ripped
a cabinet, shear from
its place above the
silverware drawer
for coming out of nowhere
and smacking into his forehead.

You should have seen
the other guy.

Well, it took me 12 plus
hours—taxi, shuttle, plane—
shepherding my kid
from one coast to another
(met with pity or disdain
from my fellow travelers,
and nipples cracked to
bleed, sweat soaking through
my shirt in crescents
beneath my breasts).

And when I finally arrived
at my childhood home
it was warm, and kind,
to be with my siblings.

I was tired. I helped
with dinner, but I forgot
to put the cheese on
the damn burgers. I was
pretty sorely tired.

And when I told
my brothers what
I'd forgotten,
tail between legs,
apologies high,
wincing against a
certain fury

and they could
not have cared less,

'we'll just put the cheese
on now' they said,

that's when I realized
how I'd grown
used to being afraid
in the angry man's
home.

Frank Kearns

Dinner Party

The Budweiser ad glows out from the fifties,
in the foreground the smiling woman in lace,
in the distance the proper businessman
getting his briefcase out of the car.
*Think of all the planning that goes into meals to make **him** contented!*
My mother's degrees were in chemistry; she once
taught graduate classes. And after the wedding
Do you complement your delicious dishes by serving the best beer ever brewed?
had nine pregnancies in sixteen years,
moved into a falling-down farmhouse
out in the country to give us all space.
*It's a **fact**. Budweiser has delighted more husbands than any other beer ever brewed.*
She never drank alcohol, many days
had trouble getting out of bed,
served fried baloney sandwiches for supper sometimes,
When you plan, are you fair to yourself?
lost one son to suicide, gave up trying
to send the kids to Catholic school,
loved my father in her own way, and never
served Budweiser with dinner.

Tracey Knapp

Blonde

lipstick on the cucumbers   she couldn't keep her calves together

male gets delivered to the right box   she wasn't used to being
in the front seat

bite marks on the steering wheel   why was she upset

when her tampon is behind her ear   she can't find her pencil
fired from her job

why did the blonde fail   call the welfare office   jump off a
bridge

drive into the ditch   why did she scale the chain-link fence
break her leg

marks on her back   how did the blonde explain   have
another beer

other guys waiting their turn   the more you bang it

how many does it take to screw   a blonde at a flashing red light

crawling across the street   when is it legal to shoot a blonde in
the head

couldn't dial 911   when she wakes up on the floor

she gets dressed and goes home

Kara Knickerbocker

When Men Ask Me Why I Am Traveling Alone

I say because I want to, because I can,
because the love of lands & languages unmapped
& *speaking of love, where is your husband?*

My tongue should lie but translation gets caught on the truth—
because no other name is tethered to this passport
that I carry, & *speaking of carrying, where is your child?*

I say I don't have one, don't even want children,
because I've never felt the desire to be a mother
& *speaking of desire, you must get lonely,*

You must yearn for it, all the time then—
You're on vacation, time to loosen up
Undo that button, that grip on your purse

We do it better here in [   ],
I'll show you [   ] like a local
Give you [   ] to write about—

Hinged

There has always been the work of words in love,
Shakespeare and Neruda. Lyrics woven into music,
handwritten letters sailing across seas with their coffee stains,
voices stretching into telephone wires and long nights.

And now, the double-tap red heart explosion
like a certain assurance, connected behind two screens
under the same moon. But we still need meaningful elements
only the dance of alphabet can give, the sentences hovering in our heads—

So much rests on the three dot bubble, brimming into first lines,
one chance at romance, how the door to something more hinges
beautifully in an open embrace of expression, waiting to receive
what's on the other side
of that opening text:

I was going to blow my money at the casino
but I'd rather blow my load on your tits instead.

Tuesday at Baum Grove

I am barefoot, sitting cross-legged in that park behind Aldi's,
picking off dry skin on the soles of my feet.
You are on speaker phone, telling me how to cook zucchini
and wondering if I thought about moving in with my boyfriend yet.

I tell you about the armed robbery last night off Fifth Ave,
how two of my burners don't work,
and try to figure out how to dig the lump out of my throat.

I still remember when he told me, "Loving you is a chore."

I swish amber ale on top of my tongue
wondering where things went wrong,
if anyone would be up for the job.

Courtney LeBlanc

Promotion

I sit with hands wrapped
around the steaming mug.
My new office is freezing,
my desk just below the vents
that blow cold
air regardless of the outside
temperature.
I sit and sip
hot water—not tea or coffee,
just water.
Just the mug to warm
my hands and the liquid
to warm my throat.

Only men have inhabited
this space and I knew
it would be cold but
the requirement of layers
and a lined bra seemed
a worthy trade-off
for authority and power.

I celebrate
by ordering business cards
with my new title
printed on them.
Tomorrow I'll wear
an unlined bra.
I'll let my erect
nipples walk into the room
before me—guns blazing.

Josef Lemoine

Overshare

I love animals too but a racoon
barreled down an embankment
and tumbled under
my tires into my rear
view and I never stopped
not for the poodle
or the black and white tabby
or the six squirrels I hit
with five different vehicles
because I was racing from a middle-
aged man in a Camaro I cut
off in traffic who said he'd saw
my balls off with a pocketknife
if we're ever again caught
at a red light, side by side
and this reminded me of a summer
evening at my aunt's apartment
when I was thirteen
when she and her boyfriend called
me a virgin
threw Hershey kisses in my hair
and wrestled me on their loveseat
until I had her boyfriend
in my throat
and swallowed.

They asked me not to say a thing.

My therapist also suggests
I refrain from sharing such experiences
on first dates
but your hair and face
remind me of my mother's
on the night she confessed
she was thrust from childhood
by an uncle whom she meant

to avenge but instead lay
her vengeance upon me.
The only differences between you and her—
your teeth are whiter
your eyes lighter
and I love you.

Laurinda Lind

Detour

On the day you threaten to leave,
I find Fawdrey Road and follow it
on foot, stopping to pick up mirror
bits broken off cars in past accidents
and to pry beer tabs off flat cans
so kids can get dialysis, unless

that's another hoax and the ones
I've collected in the cupboard
will wind up dumped in the woods
with everything else the recycle
trucks downstate unloaded on
the sly earlier this decade. Things

don't always mean what they
mean. For instance, when I was
so distraught over divorce, but
now you are tribal in your ties. If
someone must go, let it be one
who bet on buyer's remorse.
A big dog barrels out of a yard
barking so I turn back the way

I came. If Fawdrey Road teaches
anything, it's that no route is right,
no track takes you home when
there may be no home left to go to.

Carapace

Your tendency
to hurt what
can't be helped

      the boy at the bar
      with the softboned
      hand who took
      you home when
      he read you wrong
      & you wrenched away
      & you pounded him down

the black snakes
that met our boat
that day at the island
& like G.I. Joe
you firestormed
the rocks with
an oar & beat
them flat dead

      in your rage that
      they'd gone so far
      past what you could allow
      alive in their own habitat

& within you
hidden &
sealed
something
sweet & sane
that wanted
the sun but

      got stuck
      down deep.

Your father
favored soldiers.

Tamara Madison

R.A. in a Coed Dorm

His young skin flowed
like liquid over his bones.
And his body made him mis-
understand. For a long time
I thought it was my fault.
But it was his body
that shut out my protest.
I no longer cared
that I found him beautiful,
that his interest had pleased me.
For he did not listen, let
his body cover mine although
it hurt me. There was blood
and I knew it was all wrong.
He paid me later, with a visit.
I watched him there,
on my roommate's bed,
his hands pressed together
like a butterfly's wings,
his eyes locked on the carpet.
There were no words.
When he left I heard again
my mother's warnings
about the weak, helpless
bodies of boys.

Tony Magistrale

Dora Maar

I wasn't Picasso's mistress; he was just my master.

— Dora Maar

How then to discern   her place
in between successive wives
for once not just another conquest

                                    but an accomplice

the only paramour
who could match him in mind
and temperament
                            loved enough
to envision herself   someday
                                    inside staid museums
hanging by a thin wire,
            whole chapters
devoted to their life together
in psychoanalytic biographies.

But they must have both known

        he would leave   her

to wander their Parisian apartment   alone

surrounded by images of   her own
                                    tortured face, weeping Magdalenes,
a framed mirror on each wall,

only her books open behind closed shutters.

But what insight into   that face!
cracking it   to spill out her   howling striations
portrait twisted
                                    into immodest revelations.

Did she prove Muse-worthy because

                       suffering

    was so close to her surfaces,
or was it the painter, his genius

acute to the point where he   foresaw

lost lover, refugee from aborted friendship

anticipated the profundity of her   future sorrow:

              I want my face back

fragmented   aquamarine   self-effacement
fractured
into   cubist   pieces
    until   at last
                      her every day

caught up with his prophetic pictures,
kohl-lined
        rivulets
watered by years
             and tears of salt and birds,
carved eddies
      through viscous paint
the consequence of   a cruel   breaking

her canvas finally

                        done.

Tough Questions

Yood says, *Go ahead, ask her a tough*
question. Ask her to tell you
where she lives, her telephone number,
or what she just ate for dinner tonight.

I'm not at all certain how to respond
to Yood, this friend and guest of my parents,
who cajoles me to join with him
in his wife's humiliation.

I know there is some serious wrong here,
recognize it inside her darting, furtive eyes,
the deliberate struggle it takes
to fumble out a coherent reply.

We end up sitting in awkward silence
because although I'm only seventeen,
I'm already plenty adept at steering clear
of random adult domestic bloodletting.

What occurs to me only now, many
years later, is that the toughest questions
always went home with Yood,
and he had run out of answers.

Betsy Mars

Kindling

You come to me like summer,
old fireworks, sparklers,
chips of cured mesquite,
hickory, apple wood. You feed me
I'll start you up, you say,
a slow simmer of *I'll attend to you,*
you won't get burned
while my life becomes nothing
but char. For months you cook breakfasts
and deals, spin out the line,
buy that special string to bind
the turkey, deep-fry,
another Thanksgiving
alone. I look on from afar
as you and I become characters
in a slow-motion scene, another inferno
I keep kindling. You rub together a couple
of sticks to keep it burning,
throw on a little gas, some liquid smoke
for flavor—pretend it's food,
pretend it's something
to sustain. The joke's on me:
I swerved out of my lane. Now
just more wreckage, dwindling
smoke in the rear-view mirror.

JL Martindale

Snake

On Independence Day we burned black pellets
that lengthened then slithered and squirmed
on cracked concrete until they crumbled into black ash
and disappeared like the overextended tip of his Marlboros.
Dad didn't need a jack to work under a car, able to slither beneath
with his tools beside him on an old quilt.
I never learned to fear the hiss and shake like normal kids.
Instead, I was fed barbecued rattle snake.
It tastes like anything else cooked naked in fire: burnt.

Ode to My Taint

For my dearest in-between, that t'aint the front and t'aint the back — punchline,
perennial perineum, neglected necessity invisible until…

1.
Dr. Z: arrogant deliverer of infants running late wields scalpel.
Nurse cries, "But!"
Doctor, set on proving he was involved:
like sadistic wish-fulfillment of every man who tried but failed to
break me.

How simple it was for him to touch scalpel to stretched perineum
claim he's saving me from worse
skin separates like zipper dropped.
Laughs when I ask him to at least let me hold my baby
while he sews me back together.

Who else could I turn to when the stitches loosened,
sliced taint reopening like a mouth ready to shriek?
He shakes his head. "Can't restitch dirty places," he says.
"Just keep your legs closed."

I mourned me with you with your black Frankenstitch mess,
swollen flesh breaking restraint.
Healing from the violation of entitled men,
bruised bloody like misses from jack-hammer fuckers.
I took mirror to Epsom salt tub and sobbed over what they did to
you
over what I let become of you: Frankensnatch monstrosity,
burning searing end to end of me.

2.
Skin heals over but the pain remains.
Three years passes fast for new moms: I still keep my legs closed.

"Reconstruction," the new doctor says;
his eyes reflect my sadness and maybe fear.
Another dividing of in-versus-out, front-versus-back.
Another opening and breaking apart,
but this time, I must sleep through it.

This time you have so much scarred tissue to cut and scrape away.
Saving you is the only way to save myself, but I am afraid!
The good doctor says there's no guarantees this will even work.
What skin remains is already too thin; this time I am re-sewn too tight.
Pieced together, rag doll: fourth-degree episiotomy
clit to rectum connected by new stitches, curved crooked
like a question mark
where bubbled-scarred skin had to be cut out.
I almost refuse to save you; it seems too much a risk
for no more than a maybe.
But you are more than a punchline.
Masterful healer, connecting legs and orifices,
you keep me together.
We heal and the physical pain is mostly gone.
But still, I feel monstrous for letting you take so much abuse,
so I am ashamed of you, of us.
I stay in the habit of keeping my legs closed.

3.
You are no longer the edge of honeysuckle flower,
lapped and worshipped by lust-hungry tongues
but a vine of thorn-torn flesh, blooming scars
that map what I now know to avoid.
You are fragile divide, tender thin-skin hero.
Cattle brand of motherhood,
of all the hurts of past crimes surfacing
from the birth of child and emergence of a new self—
broken but resealed, repaired, recovered:
monstrous   r e c l a i m e d
still mighty and tainted
woman.

Afterbirth

Swaddled baby finally sleeps after hours of shrieking.
Hours of comforting: failed.
Holding, shushing, kissing, crying: bled me dry.

My hair, crusty with drool,
with milk, with the grease of exhaustion
and this growing sense of dread.

Breasts ache despite being empty.
Scars throb like ulcerating wounds.
And I'm tired. I'm so unbelievably tired.

Husband: home from work: he claws at me.
His touch demanding, unsympathetic, begging:
hands on my ass; hands on my tits.
His presumptuous kiss lingers too long;
starved, self-entitled lips press too hard
and that over eager tongue forces its way in.

I want to lock my body, hide it away and weep.
I want to find a dark hole in which to die.

I tell him this. And I cry.
I cry because I cannot stop the baby from crying.
I cry because I feel so lonely, deserted
in this hollow hell called motherhood.
I cry because he doesn't get what the "big deal" is
I cry and I tell him this, but I don't think he hears me.
His desperate digits still dig at my flesh.

He says, "You don't have to do anything.
Just lie there and pretend
you are dead."

Ally McGregor

Hatching Hot Wheels

I regret not swallowing the toy
car the boy in grade school
would drive up & down
my body during recess—plastic
wheels speeding on the spaghetti
junctions of my spine, blowing
past stop signs in the creases
of my arms, refusing to use his blinker
as he did donuts around my thigh.
I once buried the car in the playground
sand, then sat on top of it—muffled
the engine with the frills of my skirt—
a mother bird suffocating her young.
He brought two the next day.

Now, cars still stalk me—
so close I could draw
on their dirty windows
with my fingertips—the drivers
decorating me with whistles
like flame stickers on my ribs—
impervious to the glares I carry
as pepper spray.

I want to regurgitate cars
in their faces—force-feed
vehicles down their throats
so I can joyride inside their stomachs,
floor-it up their esophagi
until panic nauseates them—
until they fear they might die—
because I've turned off my headlights
& it's night
& their houses are two blocks away
& they're alone.

But instead, I rev their satisfaction
with my reluctant smile, a checkered flag
that fuels them to speed away,
& they win the race
& they eat cereal out of golden trophies
& I'm back in grade school
being run over.

Cat's Cradle

The sidewalk is a runway I sprint down, my high heels clicking
like detonators counting down hours, minutes, seconds until nightfall—
until my shadow contorts into a cat—claws tapping on concrete,
whiskers twitching, ears vibrating at the ring of a faraway dinner bell.

The threads of my sweater catch on nails protruding from fences,
scarring my arms with bloody marks—olfactory tracking chips
for wolves to follow—my skin a perfume bottle nozzle spraying
trepidation into the air (it's vanilla-scented with notes of salt).

I can no longer distinguish the plumes of car exhaust from hot breath
blown behind my ear—can't determine if I've stepped in a puddle of water
or drool. Was that an ambulance siren or a howl behind me?

Streetlamps illuminate a pack of men blocking
a stairwell—their canines ricocheting moonlight.

My collar tightens,
the yarn twining
around my body until I'm folded
into a labyrinth—a cotton maze
for their gaze to permeate.

Eyes dilated in the darkness—apertures scanning for exits—
I flinch at whistles: lullabies sung in pet cemeteries,
cradles & coffins sewn from domestic animal bones.

I recall the missing posters plastered to telephone poles—
the cats found dead each year on neighboring front lawns,
feline bodies splayed for involuntary vivisections—
& I wonder:

am I wearing a cardigan
or an unzipped body bag?

Sarah McMahon

I like it cuz it's pink

cotton candy   bubblegum   roses and   rosé
flamingos   grapefruit   lollipops   half-washed
blood stains on a pale pink thong
my lips   his lips   her lips   kisses
Pink Panther   Pink   Floyd   pretty-in-pink
Valentine's Day heart-shaped declarations of
luv u 4ever babe bmine

I like it cuz it's pink he said between my legs
like a good boy
kissing it
licking it
flicking it
none of it felt great but I also didn't hate it
liked the way his mouth tasted after we finished

pink eyes   pink lies   the pink t-shirt I was wearing
when he promised me *I will love you forever*
the way his mouth quivered
the way my spine shivered
the way I learned words don't mean a damn thing

there's a rare pink river dolphin in South America
endangered by humans dumping shit in our water
opening our mouths and closing our eyes
surprised
when we see something gorgeous
surprised
that anything we do could lead to our demise

I like it cuz it's pink I whispered in his ear
the Christmas he bought me a beryl stone necklace
shaped like an *S* for my name
he thought I'd adore some narcissistic jewelry
and I do, or I did before I threw it in the river after he left,
stomped on me like a pink starburst wrapper
stuck to the sole of a shoe
spit chewed and swallowed like a stork swallows fish
whole and squirming all the way down

97

he promised if I jumped high enough and dove into him
I'd find a rare pink river dolphin swimming in his chest
I like it cuz it's red, he whispered the night
he carved out my heart and bit it
his lips turning pinkish like they always did
when I kissed him with lipstick

pink matter   pink salt   pink lemonade
pretty-in-pink Valentine's Day heart-shaped
declarations of *luv u 4ever babe bmine*

Dave Medd

No Matter How I Set Him Spinning

flying into a slug's orbit
   skim pebble bouncing
     grit in your eye
a rolling drunk coin broken token
   never to share
shatter stick twirling
   (one shaft dressed
     with a polished ramshorn
       for ploughing cornfields)

severed paw gyrating in my lap

no matter how I swat him away
   with a trick of the wrist
he wings in under my petticoat
   (a heron's grey parabola)
snapping at silver wishes
   in bubbling light

skittering over my fragments
   heaped against harm
jumping at moon shadows
   bottle of sad rag perfume
my white bodice
   itching with shorn hair

broken fly revolving
he shudders grit in the cogs
crashing his gears till my tears
oil his juddering mechanism

And I must take him
   lacerated by wild tusks
clawed, gored,
   split face pocked
breathe on my oils and ointments

distil my skin's balsam
salve his dear infection
knit up the torn
wet edge of his horizons

José Enrique Medina

Police Interviewing the Rape Victim

If they ask you what it was like, say it was like a shipwreck
that never stops sinking to the bottom of the sea.
Tell them you were both inside the destruction
and outside of it. Confess that each time
he approached you, you left your body,
since you didn't want to be both a victim *and* a witness.
Don't mention it's been going on since you were six.
Some secrets weigh less in the dark, some bones rattle less
under the weight of a lock and key. If they ask
why you didn't run away, point to your legs, submerged
up to the knee in concrete. Explain that a body, turned part block,
sinks faster when thrown into the ocean. Describe,
if they'll listen, how beautifully bubbles left your mouth
when you looked upwards, hoping someone would reach
down and pull you up. When they say *It's your fault,*
fling the door of your heart open, let all the darkness come in,
accept everything bad that's happened to you.
It's just night, after all, and you're accustomed to the night.
Besides, if you're ever going to step outside,
if you're ever going to breathe the air again,
you have to, first, unlock the door.

Barbara A. Meier

Memento Mori

Where I can ride off into the sunset like Clint Eastwood and sing
Solitary Woman like Neil Diamond.

The onion skin lies like a pillion on the cold bone tile.
The green of one single spinach leaf occupies the corner
where the cupboard meets the shelf. Pale squash seeds
ride the cabinet door, while saddlebags of crumbs
are squatters on my kitchen floor. The broom and the dustpan
stand piously and proudly, judging me from the corner by the door.
There will be no retribution for this dirty tile,
 no broken dishes, or upended tables.

The utensil drawer, a wilderness of knives, flashing silver
in the kitchen light, tailings of forks, and soup spoons
in a mare's nest with serving spoons.
The forks will not be placed precisely upside down
so the tines will not jab the painted drawer.
There will be no condemnation of the disorder
in my utensil drawer, no thrown down silver
yanked out by angry hands,
No gauntlet of rage, flinging spittle in my face,
in the hospital parking lot.
Nor do I have to listen to the muttered showdown,

for now, I am a solitary woman no longer riding
his pale broom across my kitchen floor.

Mycah Miller

On Shaving Razors

girlhood is
being taught to turn
the razor on our
own skin, bubbly
and soft,
because we are asked
to. girlhood
holds the razor
blade, the
blade. there
is enough pink
in just my name
to wield sharpness
and make soft
from it. to show
the next girl
how to hold both
in her palms:
an offering and
a weapon, her
skinned softness
holy sword and
every honed edge
a libation.

Caridad Moro-Gronlier

At Least I Didn't Rape You

The wine we shared did it. He leaned
in and offered me some killer advice

because we both turned to look at the brunette
who passed our table on the way to the bathroom—

> *Since you're into chicks, you might as well*
> > *think as if you had a dick.*

> *You have the power of preemptive strike*
> > *just follow her into the john.*

> *Wait until she leaves the stall then push her*
> > *against the wall and take what you want.*

> *The truth is most guys won't admit it,*
> > *but we'd knock you down*

> *if we had our way, spread your legs and plunge*
> > *ourselves into any pussy we wanted.*

I consoled myself with all that could have been worse
than discovering he was the kind of man

my father would have loved for me to marry,
the kind of man who considered a woman nothing

more than split and cleft, orifice, cavity,
study in absence, a maw, a void,

worse than my girlhood, the litany of less
than my father hammered into me

his words exhumed, corroborated
by the pick and spade of his confession—

Hija, a key that opens many locks is a master key,
    don't be the slut with the busted deadbolt.

I'd rather kill you than let you
    turn yourself into a whore.

At least I didn't rape you!
    Don't you know how lucky you are?

Leah Mueller

Texas Midlife Crisis

Dear Ericka:

Three months have passed since you
sat in your small American car,
faced a red and white-striped barrier sign
on a dead-end road outside of Houston,
shoved a gun barrel underneath your breast,
pulled the trigger, and died without bleeding.

Your aim was so good that even in death,
you knew how to lodge the barrel in the spot where
your bones would collapse like a planned demolition,
and there would be no spray to clean up later.
For a week, your husband refused
to look in your car for the bullet
and thought it was still lodged in your body,
already scheduled for cremation.

Post-funeral, I asked to see your car
since it was the last thing you touched
before you texted "goodbye" and pulled the trigger.
He had parked it casually in the garage,
after he pulled his Datsun 240Z out into the driveway,
and washed its exterior clean of debris.
Its body shimmered in the driveway now
like a polished silver gun barrel.
He always did love that car
and was glad to have an excuse to drive it again.

The two of us opened the door of your vehicle
and peered inside at the cushioned seat
where you deliberately took your last breaths,
noted its puzzling lack of any human remnants.
For a moment, he seemed almost
like you might imagine a grieving husband to be—
his breath shortened, and he ran his hand
across the underside of the driver's seat,
and finally said, "I found a hole."

With one forefinger, he traced the bullet hole
like you might examine a tiny wound
that had inexplicably failed to heal.
He ran his other hand under the seat
but came up empty, shook his head, and said,
"The police must have taken the bullet."

Later we drove a mile from the house
to the place where you died, and your husband
kept getting lost. He complained that GPS
had failed to store the data, but that it was more fitting
for us to drive aimlessly, as you had probably done.

I doubt if you drove aimlessly—
you had probably scoped out the spot months in advance,
you had already compiled a funeral music set list,
changed your life insurance policy, and sent farewell flowers
that were scheduled to arrive at your house
after your husband discovered your body.
It wasn't necessary, because all of his friends sent flowers—
they arrived continuously for a week
until they covered every surface in the house.

Your husband took three towering racks of sympathy bouquets,
placed them strategically in a row beside the sign
that marked the place where you had died,
then took a rapid-fire series of photos with his phone.
I wondered why he couldn't seem to stop texting
everywhere he went, even when he was driving,
until he was finally at your funeral
and had to place his folded hands in his lap.

As soon as the memorial was over,
we dined at your house on baked beans and white bread,
and everyone dove right in, except for one of your co-workers,
who stood at the side of the group, refusing to eat.
Your husband mingled, phone in hand,
pressing the tiny buttons with earnest concentration,
while your adult children cried in the corner with their father.

I argued politics with Texas Republicans
and counted the hours before I could go home,
because everyone had forgotten how to grieve
in the middle of so many electronic diversions,
and I'd forgotten how much I hated Texas.

You were nowhere in attendance, even though
your photos spun in circles on the television screen-
you with your husband, standing on your lawn
in front of the "sold" sign, you and your daughter
before you quit speaking to each other,
even a couple of photos of the two of us
that I had deliberately forgotten.

We hadn't seen each other for ten years,
and I'd never met your children, not even once,
because their father took them to Mexico after the divorce.
You were goddamn well not going to subject yourself
to the crass indignity of another divorce,
you much preferred to die instead.

The joke is on you, however,
because your husband never found the bullet
and doesn't know what to do with your ashes,
so he keeps them on a shelf in his closet.
He announced on Facebook a month later
that he was in Love, then posted photographs
of himself, grinning hugely as he stood with his arm
around a prettier woman, and I finally realized
why he did so much texting after you died.

If I were a gun-toting Texas Republican
I would suggest that your aim was cockeyed,
and you shot the wrong person, but I've
never held a firearm, let alone pulled a trigger,
and I don't recommend it to anybody.
I wish you had spared yourself, however,
and sued your worthless husband for everything,
left him penniless and bleeding in the dust.

I always thought you were the survivor,
hiding behind the cactus with a pistol,
that you would bravely fight your adversaries
until, exhausted, they finally surrendered,
and I was the one who would either make a mess
or miss the target entirely.
Yet I am alive, on a drab October evening
at the beginning of the Northwest rainy season,
staring at my own winter from the other side of the barrel,
and I have no plans to leave here any time soon.

I understand why you can't answer this letter,
and hope your death is like the vacation
you kept denying yourself when you were alive.
Your daughter took a photo of herself in her underwear
and posted it as her profile picture on Facebook,
so life does continue, and you really can't blame it
for that. If you have the chance,
wink at me from the clouds, and in your next life,
please stay the hell away from Jeremiah and Texas.

Love, Your Sister

Mish Murphy

Ants

You came home late, sweaty, dressed in your uniform, carrying your
duffle bag, and I told you I'd gotten rid of the hundreds of ants that
were swarming over the fat in your breakfast frying pan that you'd
left on the stove. You responded that I didn't appreciate all you
did for me, paying half the expenses, taking out the garbage, and
mowing the lawn.

Then *I* said that I hadn't signed a contract to be a Stepford Wife, so
why did I have to scrub your greasy pans? And that the ants were
crawling over me by the time I finished, and I had to spray Clorox
on them like an ethnic cleansing—

and you yelled that I was trying to poison us all—

and as we continued to argue, out of the corner of my eye I saw
an army of ants sneaking into the kitchen from a crack under the
window,

darkening
        the kitchen
                counters
                        in
                            a
                                gradually

                                        swelling

                                                line.

Global Warming

the hottest summer in forty years
Your clinical depression, he says, *is not my problem*
AC down at work and eighty in my office
fruit, fish, front lawn, kiss them goodbye
You're a taker...take, take, take
the sins crawl lightly out of my sinful fingers
I'm not jealous of the dog
even clean sheets smell like body parts
I've asked him not to drive in two lanes when I'm in the car
my evil thoughts, those wretched ants
he is yelling like a Shepherd barking at the garbage man
I want your birthday present back
when he sweats all night, but won't turn the air on
to cook frogs painlessly, start with lukewarm water
You never loved me, you just used me
this is not the luscious garden I planted last spring
swimming in diesel fumes, polluted air
and gradually increase the temperature to boiling
my friend Linda says, *Everyone has cancer*
he's one of those old men they'll tear the car keys away from

Risa Mykland

While I Was Driving Him Home

a man who should be grown tells me
my abuser would have blessing in my church
the steering wheel has never felt so merciful
holding my hands in camaraderie
the rear-view mirror says to me
nothing in view is inspiring
my tongue drowns in honey

not standing up for myself sounds like
agreeing with a man
when he says I can continue to be hurt
and that is okay with him
says my destruction doesn't compare
to my abuser's hypothetical need for community

my survival agrees with him in the moment
but now my tires scald this man's name
the mirrors reflect the road behind me
as flawed destruction
angry burial
every year in my life before this
has had something wrong with it
and this is all I can see some days

love that doesn't hurt
is a place I've never been to
but I'm steering my car towards it
and someday
remembering won't hurt anymore
and I will stop driving

Roses Are Red

Risa?   the him here asks, in this
cafe, fallen dust shedding like a cocoon. He sheds it the way he
always has, shrugging responsibilities and consequences away, then
repeating like a broken record of a man. He told me he didn't have
sex with her. My hands lose their nails and crack open like red
roses. My teeth all fall out at once.

I don't think we've met. I say,
What would you like today?   In these nightmares, his
face grows red. His features are sharp. Not handsome, but drawn,
like a blade. He grabs my wrist. We are then back at that party, that
night, and his lips say in a whisper,

It's okay to kiss me.   My tongue turns green,
unseen to anyone but myself. I kiss him back. This moment, I still
live in it sometimes. Rose petals drip to the ground from my hands.
I remind myself: this is only blood. I scream into his mouth. I ask
him over and over what he wants. He says,

A black iced tea with no cream.   I pour the sugar jar into
his mouth. I wonder how much fear has leaked out of my eyes. Days
later, she told us what had happened to her, drunk, in my house,
without any kind of "yes." The party turned into a crime scene. The
love there dissolved into disgust.

What is your name for the order? I can't remember it anymore.
In this he is speechless. He is eyes that say, "how could you?" and
in this is rape culture. His fingers hold her like the point of a gun,
becoming bruises on her shoulders, he gets mad when I call him a
rapist, and takes it out on everyone but himself. He says:

We were like brother and sister.   My cracked rose-red hands
have coated the register. His fingers are rose trimmers. I ask him if
he would like a receipt.

Your drink will be ready shortly.   I say. He lets go of my wrist
and his mop of hair swings away from my register. He waits at the
end of the counter. I wake up looking for the iced tea.

Robbi Nester

Screen Door
To Leslie

Chipped green door, old grass losing its spring under the foot.
Heavy, too heavy for the frame. Banging each time it closed.
We were two little girls, Playdough underneath our fingernails.
The screen door was awkward for a child, not flimsy like the others
on the block—stodgy, dodgy, opening with a shriek. It matched
the green door in its forbidding stiffness. Hard wind lashed, smashing
the screen door, slap, out of your palms, sent it spinning across the lawn,
shards of glass and twisted metal. Cyclone, my father touching down,
sweeping everything away. He grabbed your arm, another person's
child, no barriers, and whipped you while I watched and wept,
at once grieving and relieved that someone else
could share the burden of his rage.

Dion O'Reilly

Some Guy

He could barely get it in. I was so young
and dry. *I'm gonna fuck you,* he chanted
like a pep talk as he pushed.
I'd agreed to this coupling
in his closet-sized room because
he was named Guy, and I liked
the idea of that: *My first guy*
was named Guy, I would say
like a child's excuse
for breaking something.
He was my next-door neighbor
at Pleasure Point. Surfing
had shaped his trapezius
like flesh wings. This also stirred me.
I think I thought men closed
the wounds in a woman's body.
But when it happened, I felt the ache
of seeing the moon up close
through a telescope,
knowing I'd never touch it.
My mind wandered as he
drilled and pumped.
I saw irrigation pipes
I'd jammed together on the ranch,
then pulled apart with a twist
to move to different fields.
The next day, he saw me
in my yard lifting a trellis.
I knew—it was almost telepathic—
if I raised my arms, he'd be cruel.
Your armpits are too wide,
he said and walked away.
I felt like a vase in the home
of a hoarder when I needed
to be prized on a mantle.
Proud of itself. Picked up and polished.
If I couldn't be that I wanted to shatter.

Sasquatch Hunter

My housemate, Jon, told me how
he'd lay out a plaid blanket in the Olympics, uncork
a French vintage, pull baloney and pork skins
from a paper sack. Then fuck his girlfriend
hard as he could, to attract—how he loved telling me!—
his beloved Big Foot.

Such eagerness when he displayed his pictures.
Caressed them with his blunt thumb—oversized prints
framed in clawed wood. Ferns and cedars marked with arrows
pointing at nothing.

There he is, Sasquatch, he'd sigh,
the air brightening around his face,
joy buzzing in the flies, the tap tap tap
of the willow on the windowpane.

And, although I saw nothing in his photos, I loved
to watch him pulse with all the gods
of war and marriage, hell and volcanism,
whatever gods there are who make us
dream of brighter deities.

But he turned violent one day. I fled from his machete
out the bathroom window, snuck back with my best friend,
loaded my books in a VW, never
saw him again.

That night, in my distress, I slept with Phoenix, a man who took
what form he needed
to capture a girl. Years later he told me:
*I knew I'd have you, Dion, if I turned into a beast
of your imagination.* Of course, those weren't his words.

What he said was, *You set a higher bar.* Whatever.
He left me empty on the sidewalk—a chalk outline
facedown on cement.

For decades I visited the spot like a cop
who couldn't leave a cold case, like
there was some secret kept from me.
Some conspiracy targeting
me like night sweats or chilblains.

I thought maybe there was a morgue
where I would find my young face scattered with freckles,
my bluish skin, blue eyes, bruisy luminescence,
a kind of sleeplessness stuffed beneath my lower lids,
and Phoenix will have tagged it
with small forensic descriptions
of reasons we never touched,
never sent our animal stink
into an empty land.

Zoom with an Ex Who Treated Me Like Toilet Paper

Somehow it's right to see him
like this. Flicker on the wall
of a famous cave. No substance
except the life I lend him.
We cry as we must.
The world outside,
too bright to see. Too hot
to live in. My neighbor's house—
ashes and a chimney. His co-worker,
on a machine to breathe.
These days, my ex grows rich
constructing towers for Amazon, hiding
their nails, joists, and purple glue.
He believes in biomimicry—
the shape of a double helix,
the golden mean.
I listen and listen,
hear the sound of history
like water under a street
rushing from a broken pipe.
He says he's *a good man*
who made a few mistakes.
When I mention my husband—
a lull perceptible
to only the most precise instruments.
Tonight, before we spoke,
I oiled my face, aimed a light
on it. He noticed
my haircut. Let me just say,
I didn't fear him forty years ago
when I met him,
but I should have. His tipped chin, a trapdoor,
my whole life fell into.
Can I drop one last bucket into this darkness?
Every time he speaks,
my face disappears.

Loretta Oleck

Cancer

The restaurant is out of the way, in a two-hundred-year-old barn.
We share a pot of mussels and most of the shells are stuck shut—
the dangerous ones.

We know well enough to leave them be.

You are a philanthropist raising millions of dollars for Saint Jude,
Ronald McDonald House, Hole in the Wall, spending countless
hours and dollars helping children with cancer.

When I ask what was the driving factor, you share that your family
has cancer markers and many have died.

Bad genes, you say, *very bad genes.*

Did you have cancer?

No. Did you?

I hesitate before spitting out the truth. *Yes. But I'm fine now.*

Mussels with the stuck-together shells pile on the plate.

I am no longer a date. Now, I am a patient in a hospital gown.
Weak constitution. Now you imagine me dead.

You scan the restaurant for the waitress and motion for the check.

Cancer's motives go far beyond one's health, trapping its victim
inside the most dangerous of bi-valves—
the ones with the shells that never open, the ones recognized
as dangerous, the ones carelessly and heartlessly discarded.

Starfish

We eat mussels from a bucket, and you announce you are a starfish.

You are restrained when you get to the oily broth. No double dipping of bread
for you. Self-conscious about using your soft neat hands lest they get messy.

We talk politics and you don't know the names of any politicians, past or present,
and you say you are a stupid man who doesn't understand anything.

I try to make you feel better by saying there are many ways to be intelligent—
one is through the physical.

And you like that. You like that very much.

Later, you come inside my home under the pretense of needing to use the
bathroom, but instead, you jostle me back onto the couch, pull down my jeans,
rip off my panties.

I hear my voice garbled under water.
Hey stop. Hey wait.

You say, *a clit is a steamy little mussel. I am a starfish about to eat you up.*

Now, you are a different kind of man. Now, you are the kind of man
who plunges tidy little fingers deep into broth. Now, you are the kind of man
who double dips bread and messily licks with a now-not-so-stupid tongue,

but still, stupid enough to forget that mussels instinctively thicken their shells
to resist starfish—their number one predator.

Sheree La Puma

Which Country Shall We Bomb Today?

Roughly 85 percent of mass in the universe
is dark matter, invisible material that
influences the cosmos. Here at Mother's,
a biker bar in Sunset, tables are crammed
with drunk locals. Beer creates its own energy.
I enter like a shadow fleeing its skin.
For every love match, hookup, connection,
another two, three girls, cracked open.
Love is a burning city after a nuclear bomb.
It has its own way of making flesh disappear.
This is fear speaking. I have been disfigured
by a rising tide of sexual disobedience.
A man in the corner yammers on about boundaries,
Trump's big, beautiful wall. He stares at my breasts,
salivating like he's ready to screw. I document this
on my phone before laying into him about the sanctity
of my vagina. I am here for the music. Our country
is a combat zone with whipped cream designs.
I am tired of being a target in the shape of a body.

Bill Ratner

Man Talking

My father's business suits twist down the toilet—crisp summer linens, Glasgow flannels, Donnegal tweeds, a dank swirl of sartorial waste. Kneeling on the flooded master bath tiles dredging for his waterlogged wardrobe my father hisses, *there is not an ounce of man in you. You need decorum.*

We engage in a brief scuffle, I catch him with a bolo punch to the crown, he phones the cops and has me committed. It's a kind of ritual we have in our house, like spring cleaning.

In the hospital a car cigarette lighter is mounted on the wall by the nurses' station where pyromaniacs melt wax on their bottoms and light their pubic hair on fire.

Visitors Day my parents wear badges with photos of their faces. *That's not necessary,* I say, *I know who you are (cartoon donkeys pushing warm clouds out your breezies).*

My mother informs me she's dropped out of child-rearing class. My father hands me a tiny evergreen tree made of felt. *It's a puppet,* he says slipping it over his finger and growling like a pirate, *Walk the plank,* his eyes a pair of life-ring buoys floating at sea.

When he and I argue, my mother often cries. This time she just scrubs something off her blouse with a handkerchief. She loves pretty clothes. She has bulbous Russian breasts like the domes on Saint Basil's Cathedral.

We're taking you home, my father says handing me a lunch basket. My meds have kicked in, my fears of the outdoors, the grey sun, the day, merge into a restive corner. My parents walk me to the car. I stare up at the linen sky. Thickets of leaves hover, capable of striking out at me.

I say to no one in particular, *Is my sex attached to my skeleton?* My mother begins to cry. My father spits out the car window, *Look, son, drink from the fleshy part of the passion fruit. That's what men do when we're thirsty.*

I shout back, *When you're thirsty you visit Aunt Ellie in her condo and lap up her hidden waters under her brushed silk duvet.*

Mother rolls down the window and calls my father her dirty old saint. *Thank God for men,* she says. *My doctor thinks I lack friends, but who needs them when I have the two of you?*

Kimberly Reyes

@ Planned Parenthood the Week Before the Inauguration

...grace could not come to the wolf from its own despair, only through some external mediator, so that, sometimes, the beast will look as if he half welcomes the knife that dispatches him.

— Angela Carter, "The Company of Wolves"

Plotting an Instagramable picture, dodging Cabinet and dick pics, you're going on another date with Greg, a Slovenian from Hungary who *first touched himself* when Black girls like you were still a tube and glass plate away,

> bouncing balls on clay courts.

He's not your type. Bald, but, baiting. His *ex-girlfriend* is Kenyan so he pries, kneads his fingers through your hair to ensure *all that curl,* the virtue, really grows *there,* because he needs you to know he *knows* about *these things.*

> (Like the stranger two strangers ago who asked if your father was a light-skinned Puerto Rican, which could explain why you're *so pretty,* he grew up in a Black neighborhood and also *knows.*)

Greg says you *think in binaries.* As he kisses he rubs his ring finger over your brows and collapsed boundaries to see how easily they'll smudge. *It's too much.* Thumb presses the pimple on your chin. *So you're not perfect, after all.* What? *What's wrong? I'm telling you I think you're perfect. You don't need so much makeup.*

> (The new president doesn't open the car door or hold the First Lady's hand. Even progressives feel badly for Melania. The familiar. The victim.
>
> You remember Melania is a birther.)

Cruelty is his sophistication and he *has his needs* and *needs the beauty* he kneads your *flat stomach, so beautiful,* as he grabs the fat of your upper thigh

...you can lose this quickly, you know. He grabs and grabs your hand and you keep going, daring and bargaining and begging for grace, trapped in all the muck and fluidity of the in-between space.

(Zsa Zsa Gabor died the day you met Greg. Nine marriages in nearly 100 years of performance. And *Greg* isn't his real name, he eventually confesses.)

And it's your life exposed.

He was bored at home, in a rut, and his *girlfriend*, who maybe knows, but would *probably only mind if he was sloppy*, is back home *in a hut* and, *man*, now he *feels bad*.

You *should know*, although this was play, you're an *upgrade*. She's *an unsophisticated girl, you're from New York, you're fancy.* Can he *stay*?

(They're from The City. Your city: Civilization. This new president, your old mayor tell a joke about a firefighter getting *lucky* after 9/11. At the Inauguration lunch. You can't keep yours down. You need the papers. Confirmation. The nurse understands.)

To let that fall asleep next to you, inside of you, what does the touch of it do? Truth is you don't believe in it, you constantly dare it, or are it, if it exists. Truth is, liars are the most reliable people you know

write about this, he says.

"Gross, I can't put my hands in your hair without getting them greasy?!"

Every morning, before the warming
Cream of Wheat,
a wide mane brush,
bristling struggle
stretched and partitioned my roots.

Unnatural labor, made easier over
a cool pink pomade sold to black
mothers praying to the confident, polished
brown baby girls with
perky pigtails coating its round
plastic containers.

Once my shiny head left my
mother's hopeful hands
I'd let it drop, gyrate, shake to
hear the clanging lilac barrettes
boasting hard-earned coils,
twisted in time and affection.

My mother wanted me to shine;
my pastels and pomp
swayed to clink in unison.

Eric was the approval
every girl wanted.
Every day he picked me
first, for his manhunt team.

Salt, prudence dripped
from my head as we raced
around the fenced-in asphalt,
faster than the other
girls, not afraid of contact.
Confrontation: the only way
to tag, to win. We always did.

On the last day of fourth grade
I held down a weaker girl,
her face coated in conditional
retreat and matted blonde wisps.

Eric pet my head in approval,
slowly lifted his fingers,
changed his mind.

The Weigh In

... a "given" of my existence

as the intolerable
fact that I am dark-complexioned; big-boned;
and once weighed
one hundred and sixty-five pounds ...

— But then I think, No. That's too simple, —

without a body, who can
know himself at all?
            Only by
acting; choosing; rejecting; have I
made myself —

Brooklyn, New York. Winter, 2009. (170 pounds): Jordan,
Lebanese and White American, wears disdain for convention,
courtship. On his nape, snaking up his face: A clear python
swallowing a black teardrop. Inked in prison. He can only meet at
night. On sticky Lower East Side bar stools. Under his stubble. His
unwashed sheets. Bad boy fantasy. Boston Southie. All Adam's apple,
he coos: *I beat off thinking about you yesterday. I even told my boys about
your body.* (Wow!) You're flattered. Flabbergasted.

New London, Connecticut. Spring, 2010. (-32): Chris, White
American, pulls out chairs, opens doors. Tall. Finally makes you
feel like a woman, a girl. Especially when he bends down. Shouts
at you. At home. Outside cafes. (Outside—with you!) He picks up
the tab. Holds your hand. Admires how *even your wrists are tiny*. He
talks of exes. Constantly. You meet one. Exotic (and pretty, she was
pretty, right? You hope pretty is his type), petite, Puerto Rican and
Chinese. But she gained weight. His disapproval. His head shake. He
finds you between leap years. He loves that you're *not the type to let
yourself go.*

Cape Coast, Ghana. Summer, 2012. (+7): Mani, Black Ghanaian, stares from afar. Even still, up close. Up all night, he's high on his *Obruni* prize. The *white black girl*. He's a decade younger, wading in the ancient confidence of the undrowned. The rested. All pluck. Teeth and buoyancy. *Everything here is a fight. Everyone here wants the best.* He enters the ring. Wants one on your finger before you leave. The newness of your curl and tan lines. But he's familiar with your *African shape.* Owns it some nights. Thinks that you'll see him as more than a summer. Forgets you're still playing to win.

Harlem, New York. Fall, 2012. (+5): Michael, Black American, talks over you in African-American studies. Fixes his glare after class. *A drink, perhaps?* Still, you're the *clueless voice of the middle class.* He asks you for singles to tip the bathroom attendant. He's teaching. He's light-skinned. You call him mini-Barack. But he's louder. Down-er. Explains his role in the struggle: *Dating girls browner than he desires. Browner, even, than you* to suppress his white supremacist thoughts. (This is a compliment? Yes!) This is the compliment you take.

Cape Town, South Africa. Winter, 2013. (Holding): Rudy, Colored South African, reminds: *You're not mixed, like us.* Coiled blonde dreadlock brushing his chubby arm. He's right. Righteous. The ocean never obscured his view. He shows you dusty townships. Shaded cafes of the DNC rich. You run into his old classmate at the mall. Her name he can't recall. *He used to play with Black girls. Just not an African-American.* (Perform Michelle. An opening. A way in.) His Colored girlfriend shows up at happy hour. Small, curly, curvy and caramel. It's hours before he introduces you. You appreciate everything the hyphen can erase.

Chicago, Illinois. Summer, 2013. (Not Counting): Romeo, White Italian, covers your escaping thoughts with toothy kisses. Broken-English babble of *Cappuccino babies*. Language is not the barrier. He texts pictures of pink roses and his penis. He's short. You rebuff invitations to The Navy Pier. Going out. Playing house. One glass. You're halfway through the wine, before the doorbell rings. Fermenting saliva. Salt. Rubber and worry: His expiring visa. A last chance. He strokes your skin, searches for fluency, *just like Serena Williams.*

— How her soul, uncompromising,
insatiable,
    Must have loved eating the flesh from her bones,

revealing this extraordinarily
mercurial; fragile; masterly creature …

— Frank Bidart, "Ellen West"

Kevin Ridgeway

My Father Never Taught Me Anything

other than how to saw women in two
with electric charisma that leaves us
both daydreaming in separate prisons
and all of them dying while waiting
for us to join them on the outside.
He taught me how to break hearts
by way of the art of self-destruction.
He taught me how to rob, cheat
and steal the pants off anyone
I could manipulate. He never
taught me how to drive a car
or how to ride a bike or how to fish.
I looked in his dusty dresser drawers
for artifacts that he left behind:
his 1983 wardrobe and his last
pack of camel non filters,
half of it smoked on the day
he was captured, the other half
brittle with straws of tobacco
which tasted like a very bitter
kind of silly string that is
anything but silly
and is killing him as
he battles lung cancer
in prison. He taught me
the power of mystery
and the art of disappearing.
But it all has gone down
like a movie:
one big mushroom cloud
of devastation as we drift
further into the darkness
that my father taught me.

Juliana Roth

Bar South

How I wanted
the tenderness of
them, to elbow
my double-chinned
phony laughter
against a hockey player's
body, too butterflied
at the knee to keep
shin pads from unfolding,
from surprising me
with their grace, with their
frozen skin, still polar
from the rink, which bore
the fact that there was a way for me
to breakaway
from the flow
of head faked one-timers
to change on the fly
to power forward
to be loved into
something bigger
something more ruckus
than steamed Jeep
windows, loved bigger than
here where I watched
pucks in rotation.

Tania Runyan

Dear Guy in My Facebook Comments
after "Nude in an Interior" (1935), Pierre Bonnard

I posted a picture of a painting
I loved: a golden sliver of a woman
in a doorway. Thigh, breast, hand in her hair.
These are my colors! I wrote.

I loved that golden sliver of a woman
lit with rose and mango, cerulean and wine.
These are my colors, I wrote.
Then you typed, *She looks like you.*

Lit with rose and mango, cerulean and wine,
you saw my naked figure there
and typed, *She looks like you.*
My stomach pitched, and I deleted your line.

You saw my naked figure there—
you, a friend of a friend I barely knew—
and though my stomach pitched and I deleted your line,
you wrote, *She *still* looks like you.*

You're a friend of a friend I barely knew,
just a stubbled face in a lather of avatars.
You wrote, *She *still* looks like you*
and turned the brushstrokes into sweepings of shame.

Your stubbled face in a lather of avatars
I flicked away in feeble defense.
I tried to brush away the sweepings of shame,
but I was no more than a body to you,

a flicker of sex, a feeble defense.
I posted a picture of a painting I loved.
I was no more than a body to you,
a doorway to thighs and breasts, hands in your hair.

Brianna Schunk

Poem for Dad

Why does he insist on his writing?
Why does he insist on the future, on ideas
Not yet written—major plans, each chapter
A step in the right direction
Once written, like any first draft, it disappoints.
He pushes it aside, work piling up—
The next chapter will be better, he tells me,
Once I move out, once the divorce goes through,
Once I get the money, once it's cleaned up,
Once I retire—the phrases mean nothing,
Each chapter the same title.
His pen dips into the black ink of the unknown,
Hands grabbing at dissolute matter.
Or maybe he's rewriting the same poem
With the same words
The same transitions
Hoping for a different ending.
The garbage can spills over
With unhappy resolutions.

Zach Semel

On Botticelli's *Primavera*

Rules for boyhood

Be naked
but only in the right ways.
Streak & skinny-dip
but don't make eye contact.
In fact, never make eye contact
without a diplomat's stiff

> nod, like
> reluctant husbands stuck
> together on a double date;
> deny that we are all artifacts
> of closeness: nothing but knots
> of cooperating veins.

Tell no one that you know
there are 500 plant species in *Primavera*
or that you want to study them all:
to memorize the delicate scrawl on ivy leaves,
then hug the trunks they wrap around—please,
find a way to accept that love

> has limits.
> Be thankful for being
> unnoticed—
> the pluckable root,
> the scavenger's snack
> do not survive.

When spring comes,
adapt—trade
your sweatpants
for baggy shorts; if
you bought a sundress,
let it age into wrinkles while

you tell yourself, "It's okay,
the florals will always be
this vibrant," even
Flora would've known
better than to look
like a woman

if she weren't one.

Nature is full
of contradictions, so be sure
that when the wind blows,
it whistles through you
most loudly, contort yourself
to be heard, color yourself

in toxic shades, remember:

the plant is a self-serving thing
and the forest is crowded—
learn quickly that a mere flimsy
flower cannot dig out a tree's
deep roots, can only stay close
or lean away

and adjust
to living without hungering
for light, for seeing the stars
appear like pollen
floating down from branches—
god, you will wish someone told you

what you really needed.

Someday, when you step off a sidewalk curb
to leave room for cis-boys slurring
and brawling, watch, and see nothing
but a tangled pair of stems in a canopy's
darkness, vying for a slightly longer
lick of sun

and know that you deserve better.

Danielle Shorr

That Summer I Was Sixteen

and spent most nights with a man
who had a girlfriend back home in Colorado. I told
my mom I was sleeping at Haley's. She was right
to not believe me.

He told me he had a hall pass for the summer,
inconsequential permission of other skin. We moved
couch cushions with our bodies and ate Reeses cups that melted
from the humidity. We sat on the washing machine during parties
and I stuck my pinky finger in the gap where his side tooth
should have been. More than once,
we passed out on the floor of the basement.

The house he stayed at in town had
a parrot in the living room and 9 pet rats in a cage
in his bedroom next to the mattress
we never slept on.

I looked at photos of his girlfriend on Facebook and drew him
pictures at my day job as a camp counselor to six-year-olds.
Haley's new boyfriend was 25, but didn't mind
her age, the same as mine.

His interests were suddenly my own.
When the *Dark Night Rises* came out in theatres,
he took me to the midnight premiere. I fell asleep
during the movie and woke up to the news of Colorado gutted.

We could have been anywhere but where
we were. We could have been there, but we weren't.

When he didn't love me by the end of the summer,
I was appalled. I had seen the movies and made the sandwiches.
I hated rats but let his rest in my hands. He had me whenever he wished.
If this was losing,
I knew nothing of it until now.

What is sixteen if not the act of pleasing someone into wanting you?
What is sixteen if not someone not wanting you?
Or a girl, stubborn and certain, becoming a creature
of disappointment, melting in August's wrath.

He moved back to Colorado the last week
of the month. September came and I had somewhere else
to be sixteen. We could have been anywhere but where
we were. He could have been anyone.

Love Notes from Strangers

Cost?

Boobs

It's 10
and a half

How much
are you?

How can I book
You?

Your boobs are
romantic

Sure do post slutty pics
for a feminist

Eat my fucking cock
until I cum in your mouth

U give your fuckin ass bitch,
then ask for some money like a
begger whore instead, u bitch

Probably shouldn't assume
every dude who speaks to you
wants to fuck you, I have zero interest
in some plastic-looking, tatted up chick who draws
on her eyebrows and is wearing 5lbs of make-up
keep trying to hype yourself up though with assumptions

PS
your husband
looks like
a fairy

Christopher Soden

Black Diamonds

I'm not sure how you ignited this smoldering
clod of fossil fuel clenched beneath rib staves,
layers of tense, sinewy chest muscle.
Is it radiant, stewing magma, like a vibe
from my dad, those comical goggles
he wore for astigmatism, just like yours?
His hair a lunar eclipse in November,
or the sky when God is finally gone
and through. Maybe you remind me
of a boy I betrayed. Not nearly as splendid,
I confess. I couldn't believe how easy
it was to just close him off. Another iron bandage
to slow the beating down. It is not sufficient
to say that I am bad news. Though you couldn't
find better company when grain and time
and distillation have turned your blood to ash
and molasses. I'm worse than strychnine,
frosty stillbirth on a farm where they track
cloud and tide but ask no help from the Father
of breath, of light. I can only say I've known
this since the night I made myself ask
you, since the Christmas of my first phonograph
and Superman cape. I am filled with chuckles
and snot and solace and bad songs. I am filled
with steam and smoke and teeth and clay and bones.
I am filled with catastrophe and disaster; earthquake
and hurricane, black diamonds spilling
from my lips.

rapture

i would never tell you god
my derelict dad wasn't there
someplace lost in the scalding
squall of my queer teen
manhood drenched in ferocious
tears and poison piss and blood
drumming in my cracked skull
spunk arcing from ridiculous purple
head of my bobbling cock rocket
intoxicated in the terrifying rush
of gangshower temple salty jockstrap
peeled from phil yorks cheerfully swaying
peter simmering drool goading
to sink my teeth into mark newells
flagrant ass how it jolted
my trembly bones to lather
beside them in that sublime liquid
nightmare imagining taste of rich spit
gooey tongue asshole clench mark
let me coax wobble horndance
from your dick convulsions filling me
with your gleaming phil let me suckle
milkspurt from your slit let me
grope and roar and sob knowing god
would devour me with rough
tenderness if i'd only known guys
would trust me with their secret
and fragile aperture if i'd only
gulped the cosmos fiercely
gobbling something radioactive
and unstable and astonishing

Jessica Stolzberg

Physics

Me, a stiff shoulder
He, a white coat

My injury, pulling weeds
His specialty, sports medicine

But a shoulder is a shoulder
Garden or field

He'll give me a shot
In just the right space

I ask a question
It's physics, he begins

And comes alive with pad and pen
To draw the moving parts of a joint

His eyes focus, his mouth moves
My ears prick

You don't look like someone who studied physics.

The doctor is correct
I studied Homer, in the original

But Ancient Greek won't get me out of this room
So I take the shot

And tuck his words
Behind cartilage

My shoulder heals
But it still feels the weight

Of being left to wonder
What I look like

Alison Stone

Heritage

When my father killed my mother
no one noticed.
The dead can cook.
The dead can dress their hair in tv styles
and lie back for sex, almost breathing.
They live in towns where birds
shriek like hysterics
while men decapitate the grass.
See them in the malls and doctors' offices,
all those dead smiling women
with their daughters of ash.

When my grandfather went deaf and blind
I didn't notice.
He had always been a statue,
funny and formidable in Grandma's tiny living room.
Once per meal he spoke, his lecture
landing on the conversation like a spaceship.
When he left we cleared away
the silver bones of the hen he had picked clean.

My father didn't kill my mother.
her parents delivered her, embalmed,
to his bed.
True, he could have woken her with a kiss.
She had read the books and was willing.
Instead he pressed her down with his body
and sealed her lips.
She had wine and the beloved ghosts
of relatives who praised her laundry.

As long as they can harm us
the dead do not die.

When I began to kill my father
all males knew,
just as ants pick up the signal
from a comrade in need.
Men on the street increased their catcalls.
My boyfriend left his socks on the floor.
Ghosts in my head threatened to leave.
Still, I kept on with my killing.

Then something strange began to happen
in my parents' house.
A singing wind tapped their door
and flowers in the garden shone with blood.
My mother got color in her cheeks.
Though the ghosts grabbed at her hair, I held her feet
while she pushed herself through the tunnel
to enter her life.

Daryl Sznyter

What Women Talk About in Bathrooms

How cruel it is to be punished
with the burden of population. How lonely
it is to have someone else inside you.
How whiptail lizards don't need men
to reproduce. How we would start a commune
of single mothers if only we were whiptail lizards.
How vaginas are everything. How we wish men
would stop asking what brings us relief without listening
for the answer. How what brings us relief has nothing
to do with them and everything to do with us.
How sometimes, we wish they would just leave the room
so we could have pleasure too. How vaginas hurt
when in use by anyone but ourselves. How vaginas hurt
so much when in use that growing old and unfuckable
is the unspoken relief. How vaginas shrivel with age
like dried rose petals in a bed that was at one time romantic,
but nobody sleeps there anymore to crush them into dust
and how we can't decide if that makes us happy or sad.

Kelly Grace Thomas

When the War Comes

you are black out/drunk at a party/he fucks you on a mattress/without
sheets/you run/from hands wish for arms/when the war comes/you
lose/your wine in a bottle of names/when the war comes/you are only
16 have not learned/the word *combat*/the war is here   inside/this
room/and you think/love is locking the door/you empty yourself/of
mouth/crawl from him/a smudge of body/when the war comes/you
are unarmed in soupy dark/There is blood/on the mattress in this
room/passed through the hands of many/generals they never speak
of bodies/they only blame the war

Burn the Boats

Because I believed somehow
it was my fault: I never told
anyone how great grandmother pinched
the extra chub around my waist
and asked *who will keep you
now?* Pointed to every empty man
not at our table. Told me I'm only as good
as what I can please. Hunger

my only harbor. I carried this: a body
full of broken boards
and boundaries.
I never told anyone
how my first love dropped threats
like an anchor. Warned me
what would happen
if I took on water. Sinking always slipped
between his speech. I believed
being boarded equaled boat. So I floated
for seven years subtracting

what I had for another body. Parts
of me couldn't fit inside his hands.
My first love never let me use his front door.
Instead gave me a dark porthole
to climb through. I only remember this: in bed
he would measure the circumference of my thighs.
Then beg for less. I became the smallest vessel
I could steer. Every day he climbed through
my story. Until I gathered enough

distance to choose another
name. I can't turn back.
I strike a single match.
Burn myself   brighter.
The boats that built me
smoke on shore.

Naked

He took me in tiny bites
of bedroom. He was always there.
Fed until I grew sick. My stomach
ripened.

He doesn't need a face.
Or name.

I give back garden
of blood, bone. The book
that named me. He licks his lips
as he watches. I don't believe in sin

or the many men. Liberty is sick
of being someone's woman.

Every night I take apart my breasts.
Clean my weapons. Cross them.

I sleep alone. Take my body.
But leave me words. Grieved
through grammar lust. Hollow
enough to fit inside a pretty
mouth.

I spelled my name with this war.
Carried this body. Targeted

and tender. Woman
wear your blood
on the outside.

Lynne Thompson

The Viewing

One brother said *let's make it easy on ourselves
and bury her naked.* But I couldn't. I wouldn't
dare do that to a woman who might return as haint.
I feared she'd return cursing, placing hot embers
on my head where she's still knocking around with
her orders, ominous warnings, and vague scent of
onions, a crooked thumb still pressed to my throat.

And yet, when we saw Mother last, she was laid out
in the finest final box we could afford, her mouth
pursed into a scarlet simper she would never have
simpered in life. Still, my brother's suggestion holds
a certain fascination. I think of it often. I can picture
the mourners who would have passed by her coffin
in a single, started file, whispering *did you recall
that her hands were so small, her breasts so lovely?*

Lucilla Trapazzo

Psalmody
for a child bride from the point of view of the mother

Rock-a-bye baby my cinnamon girl
it tinkles in silver your smile of milk.
Swing, my little on the seesaw
and gather the infinite plan of the game.

The hour thickens it stretches its hand.
The name crumbles. The rope breaks.
You are the queen bride. You are a child bride
my little green almond covered with gold.
Painful the violin - it screeches
it harvests the silence.

Wake up, wind bending the reeds
unchain a storm of sand and of ice.
Grab her, wind filling the spikes
let her not feel, let it be light.
Dissolve her, wind spreading the seeds
take her off flying in sunny fields
of wheat that is golden of stars and of flakes.

Open the doors tear up my womb
red is the night and crushed, amphisbaena.
Open the doors and pour in the honey
her name is written with colors and spices.
Open the doors and offer her dolls.

Open the doors tear up my belly.
Open the doors.
Open the doors.

Salmodia

Dondola dondola bimba cannella
Tintinna in argento il sorriso di latte.
Dondola piccola sull'altalena
raccogli del gioco il piano infinito.
L'ora si addensa tende la mano.
Si sbriciola il nome. Si spezza la fune.
Sei sposa regina. Sei sposa bambina
mia mandorla acerba coperta di oro.
Straziante il violino che stride che miete
silenzio.

Svegliati vento che pieghi il canneto
scatena tempesta di rena e di ghiaccio.
Afferrala vento che riempi le spighe
fa che non senta fa che sia lieve.
Scioglila vento che spargi sementi
e levala in volo in campi di sole
di grano maturo di fiocchi di stelle.

Aprite le porte squarciatemi il grembo
è rossa la notte diruta anfisbena.
Aprite le porte versatele miele
è scritto nelle spezie il nome.
Aprite le porte donatele bambole
Aprite le porte straziate il mio
ventre. Aprite le porte.
Aprite le porte.

Ben Trigg

Purpose

*If you can remove a female character from your plot and replace her with
a sexy lamp and your story still works, you're a hack.*

— Kelly Sue DeConnick

Put the fruit down. Don't offer him a bite.
He will be happier in ignorance.
You knew this about him before your own teeth tore
into fleshy knowledge.
Don't pretend you were tricked. You could already feel
the divide.
He was content with doing the naming.
Of course he was, it gave him purpose.
Your purpose was to look pretty while he did things.
A sexy lamp, if you will.

Understanding looks better on you than your spotlight ever looked on him.

Pedestal

I was once a goddess of death.
I shone so bright
I burned the soul from men's eyes.
I offered nothing.
They gave me
everything.
Death was their worship.
I asked for nothing.
I wished to be left alone.
But still the men came.
Demanding my light.
They piled at my feet, scorched husks.
I did not ask to be death.
They made me be her anyway.

Jeff Walt

I Walk My Neighborhood at Night

The mutt my ex left me
has broken free from the back yard fence.
Now I'm scavenging the streets,
still in my work boots, greasy clothes,
the paper mill's stench that hangs on me
no matter how much soap I use.
"Lucky," I shout, as if the mongrel might come running, jump up,
lick my face; as if I have something to offer besides a chain
around his neck and leftover SpaghettiOs.

I stumble through dark yards—
windows glow, boxes of private lives lit: families
finishing dinner, clearing tables, watching TV. A boombox
screeches "Cocaine"; a man yells at a woman, hands
thrashing in the air. I remember being struck by love.
What would I say if I slammed in there? What words
would change anything?

My neighbor rattles home in his car, calls his six kids
little sons-of-bitches—their small, vague
bodies like shadows, skipping circles and clapping
lightning bugs dead between their hands.

As a boy, I wanted to kill
everything smaller than me: beetles sprayed
with Aqua Net, butterflies smacked
from the bright air, wings dipped in motor oil.
In those moments, I was certain
I would become a man who could conquer anything.
I yell down a dead-end street
for a dog I know doesn't love me, a pet afraid
of my voice hard as the two-by-four I've whacked
against his rib cage, days and days chained to himself.

Ellen Webre

Brother Fool
After Marilyn Chin and C.S. Lewis

Brother
you wish to be   a witch's bridegroom
      to clap your hands
         and let rainbows manacle
            your wrists
    to the holy rock   of belonging
                      but
       here   on   earth
   your heart
   and mind   dance
         with
         incompatible
           philosophy
         with sexual   &
           literary
              vanity
      whose heels
         whet the   blades
           of loneliness
    It scrimshaws   your bones
        and the   blood-veined fingers
        your family has
    passed down
        for generations

Fool
    if you soak   in a selenite bath   light rose candles
         paint your horoscope
           across your chest
   you will invite
      crickets   into your   bed
        and their everlasting   croak of dawn
    will aggravate   the chronic horror
           of growing old
             without love

Fool Brother
                the moon is a confection
                        of rock sugar
        milk wine   screwtaped
                with anxiety
                        &
                                uncharitable
                                impatience for triflers
do not practice her song
                                unpracticed
                                        as you are
                she has seen
                        so many lovers bury each other
                                                in grave dirt
                                you have no shovels
                                        with which to claw
                                                the earth

Brother Fool
                I warn you from marigolds   & white oleander
                        I warn you   from chrysanthemums
                                                                        or you
will court the disease   you crave
                                                without antidote

Brother Fool
        there is no witch
                or wedding bed
                        or child born in a tulip
                                        for you to foster
        no daughter
                no son
                        only the house of belonging
                                you build yourself.

Teenagers Will Scream If You Love Them

We children of dark horses, the silver-tongued and claw-tipped,
the furry-tailed and horned gods of transport cry and christen
this car as holy chariot. We children of carved tools press our knees
to leather, smack boots to rubber road, hands and lips in prayer
for our hangdog mouths burbling the holy wine of bones and beginning.
We break the bread of dreams in milk teeth, hungry for divine spit
and circumstance. Here we howl, here we ride in the belly
of the morning and evening sun. The world wakes to our shrieking
and we carouse for the pleasure of our king, oh blue-eyed,
oh, ripped jeans and perfect knees, he wears a coronet of thorns sideways,
smoking cloves and clover, burning us charcoal. We spread our skin
for the rip of his carnelian clutch, bleeding crescent moon nails
when he takes our throats tender, sows seeds of black bruising, sweet violet.
We shake off sleep like dogs in water, we ribbon fingers in gold
to whip the trains raw, we light cigarettes with explosions,

you've never seen anything like this before, new girl,
feather soft egg-nester with golden yolk on your tongue,
open wide and swallow a crumbled fortune, divine sacrament
falling from His hands. Our king thinks you deserve a taste of the future.
Child, come crawling or we shall drag you in crooked, scraping your knees
in the supplication we know you crave when your eyes light in hellfire
whenever he strikes the concrete. Your smoke rises thickly
at every passing graze of his holy. He could scrimshaw your bones
right out of your body, he could rope your ankles and flay you slow.
You would still blush scarlet; you would still sing his name. He knows,
you know. Can't help but smile out the window at the scorched earth
we have razed in his honor. Can't speak,
can't say It that he wants without making it true. You bring out the ocean
in him, the sweat stuttering stammer of soft shaking in his sacrilege,
the way his hands flex from the branding your hands give. Teenagers

will scream if you love them, so give him a kiss, girlie, summon
your courage. You'll hear his voice through us, our never-ending wail.

Almond Blossom

I have spent a thousand years
picking myself out of the middle of nowhere

on an empty highway   clutching fistfuls
of fireflies to my eyes   clawing poppy

blossoms across a belly   full of rabbits
    I dripped with peppercorns   I salted

the earth   as if that would make   the mud
easier to swallow   I buried the creatures

with a pocket watch   and a dead fish
and mounds rose up   the hills   of my body

a congregation of sparrows   sang like nightingales
    as if that would bring me peace   my ghost

is mad Ophelia babbling   in swampflower
poltergeisting the highways   and waiting

for the next thud   of wooden dolls   slapped
out of my hands   brings me walnut shells

to curl into   like that could keep me safe
from waking up   again   in the cheekbone curve

of a boy   who does not know the difference
between a raven and a writing desk   between

I'm sorry   and   have some wild almonds
love   I picked these myself

you'll have to kiss me   to taste them

Aruni Wijesinghe

Revlon Super Lustrous Lipstick, Crème Color #640, Blackberry: Part II

With my mask, I controlled all of the mouth movements with my own mouth.

— *Peter Mayhew*

his thumb wipes the stain
from my lips

You know what they say,
he growls.
The darker the berry,
the sweeter the juice.

looks at the smudge
on his fingerprint,
rubs the dark
on the thigh of his jeans

my naked mouth
defenseless

Someone's Nephew (excerpt)

Uncle Edward chucks me under the chin.
"Come," he says. "Say hello to this nice *aiya*.
He has come from Ceylon to study."
It's the 1970s and almost every family has
a nephew who has come to study abroad.
I don't know this *aiya*, this elder brother.
All boys older than me are *aiya* in our small world.

The nephew sits in a displaced kitchen chair.
He is all limbs, batik shirt hanging
on his skinny frame.
He leans forward, forearms resting on thighs,
hands hanging limp between his knees.
Uncle Edward nudges me forward.
"Don't be shy. Say hello."

Aiya is thin and wilted in this hot apartment.
I trace the carpet pattern with my toe.
"Hello *aiya*," I say quietly.

Aiya extends a formal hand.
"Pleased to meet you, Madam," he says,
then breaks into an easy laugh.
My small hand disappears into his,
and his palm is cool and papery.
He pulls me towards him
until I am pressed against his bony knees.
Uncle Edward moves off into the crowd
to refill glasses and talk island politics.

Aiya smiles and asks my name.
I am too shy to answer.
He holds my small face
between his thumb and forefinger,
appraising me.
"What big eyes for such a small girl."
He fingers the sleeve of my party dress.
"Such a pretty dress" he purrs.

"Maybe when you are big I will marry you."
He leans his face close to mine,
his sour breath on me.
I can see crumbs of *murukku*
in the corners of his smile.
He narrows his eyes. "So pretty.
Won't you give me a kiss?"

My child's heart beats a canary tattoo,
my too-large eyes brim with tears.
This *aiya* is probably no older than sixteen,
but he fills the room.
He can feel me tremble against his legs.
He laughs and releases my face.
"Yes, I will marry you when you are big."
I run back to safety of the kitchen,
his laughter following close behind.
"Goodbye, pretty girl."

His words are an accusation.

Cole W. Williams

The Legacy of Nipples

Not for me, the industry standard of bra inserts—
       fabric disks to smooth and boost,
like my Barbie's looked: smooth and same-sized,
so that
when I first saw a bitch lie back after birthing
pups, for a belly rub, happy faced, I drew back aghast,
embarrassed on behalf of a nursing mother dog.*
***Appendix I:** Story of seeing my mother in the bath.

My hidden nipples are a legacy, a gift of personal
property, a bequest (handed down from a predecessor)
so that
when I was young, my mother would tell me to
hide myself (go play with the, wink wink, nod nod, Barbies).*
***Appendix II:** Story of my nipple sighting on the Slip n Slide.

Perhaps a partner (male) once told me my nipples weren't "right"
(as soft) and to "get them right" (as hard) although I grew up
being told "right" was soft and hard was "wrong"
so that
I learned about the politically correct nipple.*
***Appendix III:** Story on when my nipples betrayed me.

Perhaps a partner (female) not only hid the nipples,
she hid the entire breast infrastructure
so that
no one would know (or see) anything
she did not want them to know (or see).*
***Appendix IV:** Story on bound and disappearing breasts.

There is a meme that goes:
"Is this a butt or a set of breasts" and I fare awful
at this game—
so that
anytime I saw cleavage, I also saw a butt.*
***Appendix V:** Story on how my gendered body is a joke.

The bra has an evolution like any other
animal, how to bare the bra—a legend, its key:
          reveal one strap, then two, reveal the back band, side cup
so that
to go to the end of this evolution: the nipple itself.

Nancy Lynée Woo

I'm in Love with a Psycho

I'm trying to remember
the deep bellow of the cantor
in the Beverly Hills synagogue where
I had scrambled for something white to wear
(right after his father died)—and then,
that night, was it a grimace or a grin
when he ran his pointer finger down
the midline of my belly, and said he'd
like to cut me open?

You're in love with a psycho, he'd taunt
me in sing-song. I didn't disagree.
Was it actually true or is that just how
he saw himself? Was this a strange reaction to grief?

I loved him so chaotically, like a need
to be held and drowned at the same time.
I think he loved me the way you love a living body
at a funeral, someone to fill the space.

Wasn't he also a sweet boy—
didn't he rouse himself at 5 am
to fetch me medicine (yes, okay, his mother
urged him to do it, but still)?

His mother—so lovely and sweet,
probably the only reason I didn't become a serial killer,
he told me. Newly widowed,
she fed us latkes almost obsessively.

I met their mourning with my own.
My foggy sadness made me an easy target,
my desperation clinging to him, and him laughing,
and globbing on and sucking out my marrow.
We needed our fix, both of us. Was he cruel
or was I just the perfect kind of weak?

Would it have gone on forever,
slicing each other open to feel something
other than our own loss?

Maybe it was good, and in the end
we came to terms
with the shape of our raw wounds.
So poisonous, we had to learn
to spit each other out. Is he whole
and healed now? Am I?

About the Authors

Robin Steere Axworthy's writing is most often sparked by questions about almost seen connections and often concerns issues of how we are seen or heard—or not. Her work has been published online, and in various print anthologies, including *Like a Girl, Is It Hot in Here, or Is It Just Me*, and most recently, *Dark Ink* and *Lullaby of Teeth*. Her chapbook, *Crabgrass World*, published in March 2020, is available from Moon Tide Press.

KB Baltz was born in a Cosmic Hamlet by the Sea, a month early and sideways. She has been doing things backward ever since. When she isn't writing, KB can be found screaming into the void while working on her Master's degree. You can find some of her other work at *The Confessionalist Zine, New Feathers,* and *Atlas and Alice*.

When not teaching, **Devon Balwit** sets her hand to the plough and chases chickens in Portland, OR. Her most recent chapbook is Rubbing Shoulders with the Greats (Seven Kitchens Press, 2020). For more regarding her work, visit her website: https://pelapdx.wixsite.com/devonbalwitpoet.

Eryn Berg is a K-8 school principal who is also a poet and a mom of two teenage boys. She lives in Portland with her sons where she spends her time trying to find the least muddy dog park for her dog. A good Oregon Pinot Noir and a compelling crime show are the way to her heart.

Elya Braden took a long detour from her creative endeavors to pursue an eighteen-year career as a corporate lawyer and entrepreneur. She is now a poet and mixed-media artist living in Los Angeles and is Assistant Editor of *Gyroscope Review*. Her work has been published in *Calyx, Panoplyzine, Prometheus Dreaming, Rattle Poets Respond, The Coachella Review* and elsewhere and has been nominated for a Pushcart Prize and Best of the Net. Her chapbook, *Open the Fist*, was recently released by Finishing Line Press. You can find her online at www.elyabraden.com.

Eric Braman is a writer, theatre maker, and arts administrator living in Springfield, Oregon. They were raised in Michigan, where a tenacity for niceties and a love of nature was born. Since coming out, their queer identity has pushed their writing to explore themes of masculinity, mental health, and queer possibility. Braman's work has been published in *The Coachella Review* and on the album *By Your Side*, produced in collaboration with musician Cullen Vance. Follow them on Instagram @ericwilliambram

Christina Brown is a poet and educator living in Long Beach, California. She is the Managing Editor at Pear Shaped Press, and a volunteer writing mentor and member of the College Education team at Write Girl in Los Angeles. Most of her work centers around themes of identity, womanhood, the body, and healing. She is currently working on her first full-length poetry collection.

Tony Brown is a seven-time Pushcart Prize nominee who also fronts the poetry/jazz rock band, The Duende Project. A poet working now for over 50 years, he lives in Worcester, MA. His daily blog of poetry can be found at radioactiveart.blog, and he publishes eBooks of his work exclusively for his Patreon subscribers.

Cathleen Calbert's writing has appeared in *Ms.*, *The Nation*, *The New Republic*, *The New York Times*, *The Paris Review*, *Poetry*, and elsewhere. She is the author of four books of poems: *Lessons in Space*, *Bad Judgment*, *Sleeping with a Famous Poet*, and *The Afflicted Girls*. Her awards include the 92nd Street Y Discovery Poetry Prize, a Pushcart Prize, the Sheila Motton Book Prize, and the Mary Tucker Thorp Professorship at Rhode Island College.

Michael Cantin sips whiskey and dreams of robots from his couch in Orange, California. He has been published in *Red Light Lit*, *Cadance Collective*, and other publications, as well as Moon Tide anthologies *Lullaby of Teeth* and *Dark Ink*. One day he hopes for his own book to clutter your shelves.

Jan Chronister lives in the woods near Maple, Wisconsin. She has published four chapbooks and two full-length collections of poetry. Jan is serving as the president of the Wisconsin Fellowship of Poets 2016-2021. For more on Jan's work, visit http://www.janchronisterpoetry.wordpress.com.

C. Cropani grew up on the south shore of Massachusetts, but soon became bi-coastal after attending UC Santa Cruz, CA. Her writing began on buses, trains and planes during her travels back and forth. She currently makes brooms, binds books, and holds experimental poetry jams at her mixed-use art space in Salem, MA.

Alexis Rhone Fancher is published in *Best American Poetry*, *Rattle*, *Hobart*, *Verse Daily*, *Plume*, *Tinderbox*, *Cleaver*, *Diode*, *The American Journal of Poetry*, *Nashville Review*, *Poetry East*, and elsewhere. She's authored five poetry collections, most recently, *Junkie Wife (Moon Tide Press, 2018)*, and *The Dead Kid Poems (KYSO Flash Press, 2019)*. *EROTIC: New & Selected (NYQ Books)* drops in March, 2021. Her photographs are featured worldwide including the covers of *Witness*, and *The Pedestal Magazine*. A multiple Pushcart Prize and Best of the Net nominee, Alexis is poetry editor of *Cultural Weekly*. For more visit www.alexisrhonefancher.com.

Stina French writes erotic mystery, magic-realism, flash memoir, and poetry. She's featured in many Colorado venues, and her work has appeared in Heavy Feather Review, South Broadway Ghost Society, Punch Drunk Press, among others. She is scratching at the window of her body, writing poems like passwords to get back in. To get forgived. To get at something like the truth. To get it to go down easy, or at all. She wears welts from the Bible Belt, writes on mirrors and shower walls. She's working on the manuscript, *Also Arc, Also Offering*, a hybrid Southern-queerdo memoir comprised of flash non-fiction and magic-realist interludes.

Cecilia M. Gigliotti is a writer, musician, and photographer who holds an MA in English Literature from Central Connecticut State University. Her poem "Igor Stravinsky Awaits the Arrival of Dylan Thomas" won *Blue Muse* magazine's Leslie Leeds Poetry Prize in 2018; her other works have appeared in publications including *The Atticus Review, Plainsongs, Boudin, Outrageous Fortune, The Route 7 Review, Uncomfortable Revolution, A Feast of Narrative* (vols. 2 & 3), and *DoveTales: Writing for Peace*. A New England native, she now lives in Berlin, Germany. Follow her on Twitter (@CeciliaGelato), Instagram (@c_m_giglio), and YouTube (Lia Lio)

Stephanie Gigliozzi is a flight attendant and poet from Toronto, Canada. Although graduating with a Bachelor's degree in English Literature from York University, she has found herself devoted to the sky for the past six years. Travelling has allowed for beautiful, multidimensional, glimpses into the world and the lives of others. For her, poetry is the truest expression of those experiences. Her work is about freedom; freedom to love, freedom to fly, and freedom to be yourself, whatever that means.

Kristen Grace is an Oklahoma poet, short story writer, and copy editor. She is author of children's book *The Stepmother Who Dreamed of Feathers*, short story collection *Wings: Feminist Fairy Tales*, and poetry collections *After I Became a Tree* and *Love Letters to Women*.

Anne Graue is the author of *Full and Plum-Colored Velvet*, (Woodley Press, 2020) and *Fig Tree in Winter* (Dancing Girl Press, 2017). She has poetry in *SWWIM Every Day, Rivet Journal, Mom Egg Review, Into the Void*, and in numerous print anthologies, including *The Book of Donuts* (Terrapin Books, 2017) and *Coffee Poems* (World Enough Writers, 2019). Her reviews of poetry collections have been published in *Glass: A Journal of Poetry, The Rupture, Whale Road Review, Green Mountains Review*, and *The Rumpus*.

Mike Gravagno can't stop moving and making things: he's a pop-culture critic, poet, nonfiction writer, copywriter, and podcaster. Mike received a BA in Creative Nonfiction from Columbia University, and an MFA in Creative Writing from Chapman University. His poetry, nonfiction, and reviews can be found in *Calliope, TAB, the Gordian Review, Sky Island Journal,* and the Moon Tide Press poetry anthologies *Lullaby of Teeth* and *Dark Ink.*

Kelly Gray (she/her) resides in Coast Miwok land amongst the tallest and quietest trees in the world, deep in fire country. She's been nominated for both a Pushcart Prize and Best of the Net, and her debut book of poetry, 'Instructions for an Animal Body,' is forthcoming from Moon Tide Press in the summer of 2021. Kelly's writing has most recently been published in *The Atticus Review, River Teeth, Lunch Ticket, The Nervous Breakdown, Account Magazine* and other swoon-worthy publications. You can read more of her work at writekgray.com.

Caroline Hedel resides in Colorado and is a child welfare worker who has worn multiple hats in the social services arena. She holds a BA in Human Development, a BA in Spanish, and an MA in International Relations. She has written secretly for years and has only recently started to share her work.

Tania (Hyonhye) Ko Hong is a poet, translator, and cultural-curator, championing bilingual poetry and poets. Internationally published, she is author of five books, including *The War Still Within* (2019). Her poetry appears in *Rattle, Beloit Poetry Journal, Entropy, Cultural Weekly,* and *WSQ: Women's Studies Quarterly* (The Feminist Press), among others.

Jonathan Humanoid has been writing since 2012. He never intended to become a poet. He writes to better understand himself. He shares his work because that feeling of being alone is real and too common. His work has appeared in a number of places both online and in print. Most recently Jonathan has had poems in *Fight Evil with Poetry*'s first anthology, and he has put two DIY chapbooks *I Was Never Going to be Normal* and *Deconstructing Borderline Personality Disorder*. His first full-length collection of poetry, *Decomposition of the Living*, will be released in 2021 through Silver Star Labs.

LeAnne Hunt (she/her) grew up in the Midwest and now lives in Orange County, California. She is a regular at the Two Idiots Peddling Poetry reading at the Ugly Mug in Orange. She has poems published in *Cultural Weekly, Honey & Lime, Rabid Oak* and *Lullaby of Teeth: An Anthology of Southern California Poets*. She publishes a blog of writing prompts and apologies at leannehunt.com.

Vicki Iorio is the author of the poetry collections *Poems from the Dirty Couch* (Local Gems Press), *Not Sorry* (Alien Buddha Press), and the chapbooks *Send Me a Letter* (dancing girl press) and *Something Fishy* (Finishing Line Press). Her poetry has appeared in numerous print and on-line journals including *The Painted Bride Quarterly*, *Rattle*, poets respond online, *The Fem Lit Magazine*, and The American Journal of Poetry. Vicki is currently living in Florida, but her heart is in New York.

Victoria Irwin is the Editor-in-Chief of FangirlNation.com, founder of the podcast *Texas: Slang for Crazy*, and co-creator of the podcast *Unfortunately Required Reading*. She is also Bella Rose Mrs. Bexar County 2020 and Young American Miss International Mrs. Bluebonnet 2021. When not working or volunteering, she can be found writing in a notebook and spending time with her family.

Ryan Johnson is a teacher, engineer, and poet from California. He works to help young people make and claim a safe, just world for themselves. He wants to listen to your stories and plant them all in the sun.

Nikoline Kaiser resides in Denmark and studies Literature at Aarhus University. She has previously worked as an editor on campus and has written and published several pieces including the poem "ode to an asexual" with *Strange Horizons*. She is a queer author writing themes of family, feminism, and the natural world. She can be found on Twitter and Instagram under the @nikolinekaiser handle.

L. Kardon is a poet and parent residing in Philadelphia. Lookout for L.'s upcoming work in *Wizards in Space Magazine*, *Gyroscope Review*, and *Club Plum*.

Frank Kearns is a transplanted New Englander and a longtime California resident. He is the author of three poetry collections, *Circling Venice* (2013), *Yearlings* (2015), and *Pleasant Street* (2019). His work has also appeared in anthologies such as *Beyond the Lyric Moment*, *Like a Girl: Perspectives on Feminism*, *The California Writers Club Literary Review*, and *The Sand Canyon Review*.

Tracey Knapp lives in Berkeley, California. She has received awards and scholarships from La Romita School of Art in Italy, Tin House Writers' Workshop, and the Dorothy Sargent Rosenberg Poetry Prize. Her work has been anthologized in *Best New Poets (2008 & 2010)* and *The Cento: A Collection of Collage Poems*. Poems have appeared in *Rattle*, *Poetry Daily*, *Five Points*, *The New Ohio Review* and elsewhere.

Kara Knickerbocker is the author of the chapbooks *The Shedding Before the Swell* (dancing girl press, 2018) and *Next to Everything that is Breakable* (Finishing Line Press, 2017). Her poetry and essays have appeared in or are forthcoming from: *Poet Lore, HOBART*, and *Levee Magazine* among others, and the anthologies *Voices from the Attic, Crack the Spine*, and *Pennsylvania's Best Emerging Poets* and more. She currently lives in Pennsylvania where she writes with the Madwomen in the Attic at Carlow University, and co-curates the Mad Fridays Reading Series. Find her online at www.karaknickerbocker.com.

Courtney LeBlanc is the author of *Beautiful & Full of Monsters (Vegetarian Alcoholic Press)*, and chapbooks *All in the Family (Bottlecap Press)* and *The Violence Within (Flutter Press)*. She is also the founder and Editor-in-Chief of *Riot in Your Throat*, an independent poetry press. She has her MBA from University of Baltimore and her MFA from Queens University of Charlotte. She loves nail polish, tattoos, and a soy latte each morning. Read her publications on her blog: www.wordperv.com. Follow her on twitter:@wordperv, and IG: @ wordperv79.

Josef Lemoine is a Filipino-American writer living in Southern California with his wife, son, and daughter. In a past life, he was part of the 2010 and 2011 CSULB Slam Poetry Teams. He and his teammates were Region 15 Champions who competed in the 2010 College Unions Poetry Slam Invitational in Boston. His poetry, nonfiction, and fiction can be found online.

Laurinda Lind lives in New York's North Country. Some publications/ acceptances are in *Blue Earth Review, New American Writing, Paterson Literary Review*, and *Spillway*; also in anthologies *Visiting Bob: Poems Inspired by the Life and Work of Bob Dylan* (New Rivers Press), *What I Hear When Not Listening: Best of The Poetry Shack & Fiction, Vol. I* (Sonic Boom), and *Civilization in Crisis* (FootHills Publishing). She is a Best of the Net nominee.

Tamara Madison is the author of the chapbook *The Belly Remembers*, and two full-length volumes of poetry, *Wild Domestic* and *Moraine*, all published by Pearl Editions. Her work has appeared in *Chiron Review, Your Daily Poem, A Year of Being Here, Nerve Cowboy*, the *Writer's Almanac, Sheila-Na-Gig* and many other publications. She has recently retired from teaching English and French in Los Angeles and is happy to finally get some sleep. More about Tamara can be found at tamaramadisonpoetry.com.

Tony Magistrale is a Professor of English at the University of Vermont. His most recent book of poems is entitled *Dialogues Among Lost Tourists* and is published by Finishing Line Press.

Betsy Mars lives in the southern California suburbs where she practices poetry, photography, and runs Kingly Street Press. Her second release, *Floored*, features 27 poets from around the world and is available through her, the authors, and also on Amazon. She was a winner in *Alexandria Quarterly's* first line poetry contest series in 2020 as well as a finalist in both the Jack Grapes and Poetry Super Highway poetry contests. She is the author of *Alinea* (Picture Show Press) and co-authored *In the Muddle of the Night* (Arroyo Seco Press) with Alan Walowitz.

JL Martindale writes poetry and prose. She's honored to be included in this anthology. Her poetry has also been published with *Cadence Collective, Bank Heavy Press, Lucid Moose Press, A Poet is a Poet, Sadie Girl Press*, and more. When JL Martindale is not writing or reading, she's playing video games with her family, D&D with friends, or taking too many pictures of her cat and dog.

Ally McGregor is a contemporary Surrealist poet with an affinity for all things dark, whimsical, and strange. She often uses childlike metaphors to explore serious personal and societal issues, especially those pertaining to feminism and mental illness. She obtained her M.F.A. degree in poetry from California State University, Long Beach and currently resides in Long Beach, California.

Sarah Rose McMahon is a poet and blogger based out of Laguna Beach, CA. Her blog, *The Prosiest*, features articles and insights about running, eating disorders, writing, and mental health. She is an ultra-runner, transitioning to mountain races after competing in cross country and track at Bradley University, where she graduated with her M.A. in English in 2016.

Dave Medd was born in Hull in 1951. In 1965 he discovered folk music, Bob Dylan and Dylan Thomas. He taught various subjects for forty years and has written songs, short stories and musical dramas for young teenagers, and drafts of two children's novels. His poems have been published in *Poetry North East, Outposts, Orbis, Dream Catcher, The Coffee House* and *Obsessed with Pipework*, and on *I Am Not a Silent Poet* and *The Cicerone Journal*. He has read at The Stanzain Newcastle. He now lives and writes in Rothbury, where he also plays the Northumbrian pipes.

José Enrique Medina earned his BA in English from Cornell University. He writes poems, flash fiction and short stories. His work has appeared in *Best Microfiction 2019 Anthology, The Los Angeles Review, Tahoma Literary Review*, and many other publications. He is a Voices of Our Nation (VONA) fellow.

Barbara A Meier recently retired from teaching kindergarten and moved to Colorado. She is not too sure how she feels about it after living in Southern Oregon for over 40 years. She has two published chapbooks, *Wildfire LAL 6*, from Ghost City Press and *Getting Through Gold Beach*, which came out in November 2019 from Writing Knights Press. She has an upcoming chapbook of poetry, *Sylvan Grove*, coming out in March 2021 from The Poetry Box.

Mycah Miller is a CA-based poet, artist, and student, and was a member of the winning team of the 2018 Southwest Shootout. She currently attends SJSU as an English major. Her work has been featured in shows and publications across the US, including *Vagabond City Lit*, *Gnashing Teeth*, and more. When not writing, she can be found teaching as a motorcycle safety instructor or annoying her two cats. She can be contacted through email at mycahmillerart@ gmail.com or social media @MycahMillerArt.

Caridad Moro-Gronlier is the author of *Tortillera*, forthcoming from Texas Review Press in 2021, and author of *Visionware* published by Finishing Line Press as part of its New Women Voices Series, as well as the Contributing Editor of *Grabbed: Writers Respond to Sexual Assault* (Beacon Press, 2020) in 2020 and an Associate Editor for *SWWIM Every Day*. Moro-Gronlier is the recipient of an Elizabeth George Foundation Grant and a Florida Individual Artist Fellowship in poetry. Her work has been nominated for two Pushcart Prizes, The Best of the Net and a Lambda Literary Award. Recent work can be found at *The Best American Poetry Blog*, *Rhino*, *Go Magazine*, *West Trestle*, *The Sexton Review* and others. She resides in Miami, FL with her wife and son.

Leah Mueller is an indie writer and spoken word performer from Bisbee, Arizona. Her most recent books, *Misguided Behavior, Tales of Poor Life Choices* (Czykmate Press), *Death and Heartbreak* (Weasel Press), and *Cocktails at Denny's* (Alien Buddha) were released in 2019. Leah's work appears in *Midway Journal*, *Citron Review*, *The Spectacle*, *Miracle Monocle*, *Outlook Springs*, *Atticus Review*, *Your Impossible Voice*, and elsewhere. Her essay "Firebrand, The Radical Life and Times of Annie Besant" appears in the book, *Fierce: Essays By and About Dauntless Women*, which placed first in the non-fiction division of the 2019 Publisher's Weekly Booklife contest.

"Mish" (Eileen) Murphy lives near Tampa with her Chi-Spaniel Cookie. She is Associate Poetry Editor for *Cultural Weekly* and teaches English/literature at Polk State College. Her poetry collection *Fortune Written on Wet Grass* was published in 2020 by Whapshott Press. Her chapbook *Evil Me* was also published last year by Blood Pudding Press. A visual artist, she illustrated the highly acclaimed children's book *Phoebe and Ito are dogs* written by John Yamrus (Epic Rites Press 2019). Her reviews have been published in *Cultural Weekly, Blog of the Los Angeles Review of Books, Rain Taxi Review, Tinderbox Journal,* and many other publications.

Risa Mykland (she/they) is a poet and self-proclaimed special occasion, currently based in Portland, OR. She has two books: *Destruction Gospel* (2018) and *In The Hollow Parts of Our Chests* (2020). Find her work and upcoming features at @unexplained.orbit on Instagram, or at Risa Kate Poetry on Facebook. When not doing poetry, you can find her thinking about poetry.

Robbi Nester writes and shelters in Southern California. She is the author of 4 books of poetry, a chapbook, *Balance* (White Violet, 2012) and three collections: *A Likely Story* (Moon Tide, 2014), *Other-Wise* (Kelsay, 2017), and *Narrow Bridge* (Main Street Rag, 2019). She has also edited three anthologies: *The Liberal Media Made Me Do It! (Nine Toes, 2014), Over the Moon: Birds, Beasts and Trees* and *The Plague Papers*, both of which are available on Poemeleon.

Dion O'Reilly has spent most of her life on a small farm in the Santa Cruz Mountains. Her prize-winning debut book, *Ghost Dogs*, was published in February 2020 by Terrapin Books. Her poems appear in *Cincinnati Review, Poetry Daily, Verse Daily, Narrative, The New Ohio Review, The Massachusetts Review, New Letters, Journal of American Poetry, Rattle, The Sun,* and other literary journals and anthologies. She is a member of The Hive Poetry Collective, which produces podcasts and radio shows, and she leads online workshops with poets from all over the United States and Canada. dionoreilly.wordpress.com

Loretta Oleck's poetry and photography have been published worldwide in reviews, journals and anthologies including *The Stockholm Review of Literature, The Missing Slate, So to Speak: Feminist Journal of Language and Art, Poetica Literary Magazine, Word Riot*, among dozens of others. Her latest poetry book, *Paper Chains*, inspired by her experience volunteering on a Syrian refugee camp, became the inspiration and namesake of a full-length play to be included in the Up Theater's Renewal Reading series in NYC. Oleck is a graduate of NYU (MA in Creative Writing). She is a Pushcart Poetry Prize nominee, Semi-Finalist in the Poet's Billow: Bermuda Triangle Prize, First Honorable Mention in New Women's Voices Series Competition, runner up for the L.A Poetry Society Contest, 2019 finalist in the Jack Grapes Poetry contest and many others.

Sheree La Puma is an award-winning writer whose personal essays, fiction, and poetry have appeared in or are forthcoming in *The American Journal of Poetry, WSQ, Chiron Review, SRPR, The Rumpus, Plainsongs, Into the Void*, and *I-70 Review*, among others. Her poetry was recently nominated for Best of The Net and two Pushcarts. Her micro-chapbook, *The Politics of Love*, was published in August by Ghost City Press. She has a new chapbook, 'Broken: Do Not Use,' due out in 2021 with Main Street Rag Publishing. She received an MFA in Writing from California Institute of the Arts and taught poetry to former gang members.

Bill Ratner is a Poets & Writers Readings & Workshops Grant recipient. His poetry chapbook is being published by Finishing Line Press in May, 2021. Bill's readings are featured on National Public Radio's *Good Food, The Business*, and KCRW's *Strangers*. He is a 9-time winner of The Moth Story Slams. His poems, essays, and stories are published in The *Chiron Review, The Baltimore Review*, Rattle Magazine's *Rattlecast, Pleiades, Missouri Review Audio*, and other journals. Bill earns his living as a voice actor. Info at: billratner.com/author.

Kimberly Reyes is poet and essayist and the author of three books: *Warning Coloration* (dancing girl press 2018), *Life During Wartime* (Fourteen Hills, 2018), and *Running to Stand Still* (Omnidawn, 2019). Kimberly Reyes has received fellowships from the Poetry Foundation, the Academy of American Poets, the Fulbright Program, Canto Mundo, Callaloo, Tin House Workshops, the Department of Culture, Heritage and the Gaeltacht in Ireland, the Munster Literature Centre, the Prague Summer Program for Writers, Summer Literary Seminars in Kenya, Community of Writers at Squaw Valley, Columbia University, San Francisco State University, and other places.

Kevin Ridgeway is the author of *Too Young to Know* (Stubborn Mule Press) and nine chapbooks of poetry including *Grandma Goes to Rehab* (Analog Submission Press, UK). His work can recently be found in *Slipstream, Chiron Review, Nerve Cowboy, Plainsongs, San Pedro River Review, The Cape Rock, Trailer Park Quarterly, Main Street Rag, Cultural Weekly* and *The American Journal of Poetry*, among others. He lives and writes in Long Beach, CA.

Juliana Roth is a multi-genre artist, educator, and the creator of a web series on campus sexual assault and healing trauma called The University. She likes writing postcards. Learn more at www.julianaroth.com.

Tania Runyan is the author of the poetry collections *What Will Soon Take Place, Second Sky, A Thousand Vessels, Simple Weight*, and *Delicious Air*. Her guides *How to Read a Poem, How to Write a Poem*, and *How to Write a College Application Essay* are used in classrooms across the country. Her poems have appeared in many publications, including *Poetry, Image, Indiana Review, Atlanta Review*, and *The Christian Century*. Tania was awarded an NEA Literature Fellowship in 2011.

Brianna Schunk is a recent graduate from Wilkes University and is pursuing communication and exploration in all forms. She is a trainee with the Limon Dance Company and has recently published research with W. W. Norton and *UReCA*. Her poetry can also be found in *Sagebrush Review, Manuscript*, and the *Luzerne County Poetry in Transit* program. She is very grateful to her mentors in writing and hopes they share in her success.

Zach Semel is an M.F.A. candidate in Creative Writing at Northern Arizona University. He is an avid Celtics fan, a wannabe psychoanalyst, and a lover of all things garlicky. Some of his previous poems and essays have appeared in or are forthcoming in *DIAGRAM, CutBank, Flyway: Journal of Writing & Environment, The Nervous Breakdown, Wordgathering, Breath & Shadow*, and other places.

Danielle Shorr is an MFA alum and professor of rhetoric at Chapman University forever trying to make the transition from poetry to fiction. She has a fear of commitment in regard to novel writing and an affinity for wiener dogs. Her work has been published by MTV, *Crab Fat Magazine, Hobart, Split Lip*, etc.

Christopher Stephen Soden received his MFA in Poetry from Vermont College of Fine Arts in January of 2005. Christopher's poetry collection, *Closer* was released by Rebel Satori Press on June 14th, 2011. He received a Full Fellowship to Lambda Literary's Retreat for Emerging LGBT Voices in August 2010. Other honors include: Distinguished Poets of Dallas, Poetry Society of America's Poetry in Motion Series, Founding Member, President and President Emeritus of The Dallas Poets Community. His work has appeared in: *Rattle, The Cortland Review, 1111, G & L Review, Chelsea Station, Glitterwolf, Collective Brightness, A Face to Meet the Faces, The Texas Observer, Sentence, Borderlands, Off the Rocks, The James White Review.*

Jessica Stolzberg is a freelance writer and editor who lives with her family in Montclair, New Jersey. Some of her writing appears in *Slate, Vice,* and the *New York Times.*

Alison Stone has published seven full-length collections, *Zombies at the Disco* (Jacar Press, 2020), *Caught in the Myth* (NYQ Books, 2019), *Dazzle* (Jacar Press, 2017), *Masterplan,* a book of collaborative poems with Eric Greinke (Presa Press, 2018), *Ordinary Magic,* (NYQ Books, 2016), *Dangerous Enough* (Presa Press 2014), and *They Sing at Midnight,* which won the 2003 Many Mountains Moving Poetry Award; as well as three chapbooks. Her poems have appeared in *The Paris Review, Poetry, Ploughshares, Barrow Street, Poet Lore,* and many other journals and anthologies. She has been awarded *Poetry's* Frederick Bock Prize and *New York Quarterly's* Madeline Sadin Award. She was Writer in Residence at LitSpace St. Pete. She is also a painter and the creator of The Stone Tarot. A licensed psychotherapist, she has private practices in NYC and Nyack. For more go to stonepoetry.org.

Daryl Sznyter is the author of *Synonyms for (OTHER) Bodies* (NYQ Books). Her poetry has appeared in *Diode, Poet Lore, Harpur Palate, The American Journal of Poetry, Best American Poetry Blog,* and elsewhere. She received her M.F.A. from The New School. She currently resides in northeastern Pennsylvania, where she works as an SEO specialist, content writer, and adjunct professor.

Kelly Grace Thomas is an ocean-obsessed Aires from Jersey. She is a self-taught poet, editor, educator and author. Kelly is the winner of the 2017 Neil Postman Award for Metaphor from *Rattle,* 2018 finalist for the Rita Dove Poetry Award and multiple pushcart prize nominee. Her first full-length collection, *Boat Burned,* released with Yes Yes Books in January 2020. Kelly's poems have appeared or are forthcoming in: *Best New Poets 2019, Los Angeles Review, Redivider, Muzzle, Sixth Finch* and more. Kelly is the Director of Education for Get Lit and the co-author of *Words Ignite.* She lives in the Bay Area with her husband Omid. www.kellygracethomas.com.

Lynne Thompson is the author of *Start with a Small Guitar, Beg No Pardon*, winner of the Perugia Book Award and the Great Lakes Colleges New Writers Award, and *Fretwork*, selected by Jane Hirshfield for the Marsh Hawk Poetry Prize. Her recent work appears or is forth coming in *Ploughshares, New England Review, Pleiades, december, Black Warrior Review*, and *Best American Poetry 2020*.

Lucilla Trapazzo, born in Cassino, Italy, she lives in Zurich. After a degree in German literature ("La Sapienza" University, Rome), a MA in Film & Video ("American University" of Washington, D.C.), and continuing education in art and theater, she works as an actress, a critic, and a translator. Her activities range among poetry (translated in ten languages, recipient of different prizes, publications in International anthologies and art books, and Festivals), theater, video-installations, and literary critiques. In her works she longs for a synthesis of all the different artistic languages. Her artworks have been shown at several International exhibitions and festivals.

Ben Trigg is the co-host of Two Idiots Peddling Poetry at the Ugly Mug in Orange, California. His full-length collection *Kindness from a Dark God* came out on Moon Tide Press in 2007. He co-edited the anthology *Don't Blame the Ugly Mug: 10 Years of 2 Idiots Peddling Poetry* published by Tebot Bach. When all else fails, Ben goes to Disneyland.

Jeff Walt is a Regional Editor with the *San Diego Poetry Annual* and their coordinator for the Steve Kowit Poetry Prize. His book, *Leave Smoke* (Gival Press, 2019), was a Runner-Up in the San Francisco Book Festival competition and winner of the 2020 Housatonic Book Award in Poetry.

Ellen Webre was born in Hong Kong and raised in Orange County. She is a graduate of UCI's MAT program and has a BA in screenwriting from Chapman University. Ellen is also the social media specialist for Moon Tide Press and the Two Idiots Peddling Poetry reading in Orange, CA. Her poetry largely explores the celestial and supernatural, myth and folklore. She has been most recently published in Moon Tide Press' *DARK INK: A Poetry Anthology Inspired by Horror* and *Voicemail Poems*.

Aruni Wijesinghe is a project manager, ESL teacher, erstwhile belly dance instructor and occasional sous chef. She has been published in anthologies and journals both nationally and internationally and has collections forthcoming with Moon Tide Press and Silver Star Laboratory. She lives a quiet life with Jeff, Jack and Josie.

Cole W. Williams is the author of *Hear the River Dammed: Poems from the Edge of the Mississippi* (Beaver's Pond Press, 2017) as well as several books for children. Her poems have appeared in *Martin Lake Journal, Indolent Books Online, Waxing & Waning, Harpy Hybrid Review, WINK*, and other journals, as well as in a number of anthologies. Williams is a student in the MFA program at Augsburg University in Minneapolis.

Nancy Lynée Woo spends her free time hitching a ride to the other side of maybe. She is an MFA candidate at Antioch University, the recipient of fellowships from PEN America, Arts Council for Long Beach, and Idyllwild Writers Week, and the author of two chapbooks. She is also the creator of Surprise the Line poetry workshops. Find her cavorting around Long Beach, California, and online at nancylyneewoo.com.

About the Artists

Kia Hinton is an artist and musician who spends most of her time in Hollywood, fabricating outrageous costumes for film and TV. In her spare time, she tends to all manner of growing things from people to carnivorous plants. She is a strong advocate for social justice, gender and racial equality and LGBTQ+ rights, and has a knack for herding cats.

Kat Keller is an artist who splits her time between screaming at the sea and into the void. In her free time, she wrangles monkeys. If she likes you, she will volunteer to vanquish your minor and major annoyances. She also believes radical kindness will save the world.

About the Editors

Dania Ayah Alkhouli is a Syrian writer, poet, and editor born and raised in Southern California. She is the author of three poetry collections, *91 at 19*, *Oceans & Flames*, a collection of poetry shedding light on her experience with, and survival of, domestic violence, and most recently, from Moon Tide Press, *Contortionist Tongue*, a collection weaving into words the experience of being a Muslim Syrian woman in today's socio-political climate. Alkhouli's work centers on feminism, mental health, sexuality, identity, culture, religion, her war-torn homeland, Syria, and on grief, loss, and death. In 2012, Alkhouli and her mother cofounded the nonprofit organization, *A Country Called Syria*, a traveling exhibition and set of events showcasing the history and culture of their country.

HanaLena Fennel is a Jewish-Hawaiian American poet born on a goat farm in Oregon and raised in Southern California. She is an associate editor with the online literary journal, *Freezeray Press*. Her work can be seen in a number of online journals and print anthologies, including Moon Tide Press's *Dark Ink*. Her first poetry collection, *Letter to the Leader*, was published by Moon Tide Press in 2019.

Victoria Lynne McCoy earned an MFA in Poetry from Sarah Lawrence College and a BA in "The Power of Words: Creative Expression as a Catalyst for Change," focusing on activism in the arts, from the University of Redlands' Johnston Center for Integrative Studies. Her work has appeared in *Best New Poets*, *Blackbird*, *The Boiler Journal*, *The Collagist*, *Cultural Weekly*, *The Offing*, *PANK*, *Tinderbox*, and *Washington Square Review*, among others.

Acknowledgements

Moon Tide Press and the poets in this anthology are grateful to the following publications where these poems have previously appeared, sometimes in a different form:

"Poetess" — *A Brief Way to Identify a Body* (Ursus Americanus Press)

"Amazonian" — *Triggerfish*

"What is marriage like?" — *Rattle*

"What to Think Of" — *KYSO Flash*, Issue 10, Fall 2018

"How to Be Deposed" — *Algebra of Owls*, January 2018

"Flower-Eating Season" — *Unmasked: Women Write about Sex and Intimacy after Fifty*, Weeping Willow Books

"I Don't Want to Read a Poem About Baseball" — *Gyroscope*

"What It's Like" — *Decennia* (Truth Serum Press)

"Cousin" — *13 Myna Birds*

"Domestic Violence" — *Unsheathed: 24 Contemporary Poets Take Up the Knife*, 2019

"After the Restraining Order Expires, M. Begs Me to Meet Him for Lunch" — *Willaway Journal*, 2018

"Freeway Sex" — *Cahoodaloodaling*, 2016

"Love Letter to Holly and Sex Without Power" — *Love Letters to Women* (2020)

"The War Still Within" — *The War Still Within* (KYSO Flash Press, 2019)

"Sushi '81" — *Not Sorry* (Alien Buddha Press)

"Blonde" — *The Minnesota Review*

"Tuesday at Baum Grove" — *Pittsburgh Poetry Review*

"Promotion" — *Thank You for Swallowing*

"Detour" — *Coldnoon*

"Carapace" — *Anti-Heroin Chic*

"Dora Maar" — *Dialogues Among Lost Tourists* (Finishing Line Press)

"Ode to My Taint" — *Incandescent Mind: Selfish Work*, Fall 2017 (Sadie Girl Press)

"Afterbirth" — *Like a Girl: Perspectives on Feminine Identity* (Lucid Moose Lit)

"I like it cuz it's pink" — *I Like It Cuz It's Pink*

"Memento Mori" — "Woman's Anthology." *Carrying Fire* (TL;DR Press)

"At Least I Didn't Rape You" — *Grabbed: Poets and Writers Respond to Sexual Assault, Empowerment & Healing* (Beacon Press, 2020)

"Texas Midlife Crisis" — *Crab Fat Magazine*

"Ants" — *Mudfish 13*, 2013

"Global Warming" — *Evil Me* (Blood Pudding Press, 2020)

"Screen Door" — *Silver Birch Press*

"Some Guy" — *Book of Matches*

"Which Country Should We Bomb Today?" — *Into the Void Magazine*

"@ Planned Parenthood the Week Before the Inauguration," *"Gross, I can't put my hands in your hair without getting them greasy?!,"* and *"The Weigh In,"* are from *RUNNING TO STAND STILL* (c) FALL 2019 by Kimberly Reyes. The poem appears with the permission of Omnidawn Publishing. All rights reserved.

"My Father Never Taught Me Anything" — *Lummox 8*, 2019

"On Botticelli's *Primavera*" — *CutBank: All Accounts and Mixture*

"Black Diamonds" — *Closer* (QueerMojo, 2011)

"Heritage" — *They Sing at Midnight* (Many Mountains Moving Press, 2003)

"When the War Comes" — *Junked*; *Boat Burned* (YesYes Books, 2020)

"Burn the Boats" — *Bayou*; *Boat Burned* (YesYes Books, 2020)

"Naked" — *SOFTBLOW*; *Boat Burned* (YesYes Books, 2020)

"The Viewing" — *Luvina 57*; *Fretwork*

"Psalmody" — *Ossidiana, Volturnia Ed.*, 2018

"Purpose" — *Redshift 5* (Arroyo Seco Press)

"I Walk My Neighborhood at Night" — *Mangrove Review*, Fall 2005

"Almond Blossom" — *Voicemail Poems*, 2017

"Someone's Nephew (excerpt) — *Tell Me More* (East Jasmine Review)

"Revlon Super Lustrous Lipstick. Crème Color #640, Blackberry: Part II" — *Making Up* (Picture Show Press)

Patrons

Moon Tide Press would like to thank the following people for their support in helping publish the finest poetry from the Southern California region. To sign up as a patron, visit www.moontidepress.com or send an email to publisher@moontidepress.com.

Anonymous
Robin Axworthy
Conner Brenner
Bill Cushing
Susan Davis
Peggy Dobreer
Dennis Gowans
Alexis Rhone Fancher
HanaLena Fennel
Half Off Books & Brad T. Cox
Donna Hilbert
Jim & Vicky Hoggatt
Michael Kramer
Ron Koertge & Bianca Richards
Ray & Christi Lacoste
Zachary & Tammy Locklin
Lincoln McElwee
David McIntire
José Enrique Medina
Michael Miller & Rachanee Srisavasdi
Michelle & Robert Miller
Ronny & Richard Morago
Terri Niccum
Andrew November
Jennifer Smith
Andrew Turner
Rex Wilder
Mariano Zaro

Also Available From Moon Tide Press

Flower Grand First, Gustavo Hernandez (2021)
Everything is Radiant Between the Hates, Rich Ferguson (2021)
When the Pain Starts: Poetry as Sequential Art, Alan Passman (2020)
This Place Could Be Haunted If I Didn't Believe in Love, Lincoln McElwee (2020)
Impossible Thirst, Kathryn de Lancellotti (2020)
Lullabies for End Times, Jennifer Bradpiece (2020)
Crabgrass World, Robin Axworthy (2020)
Contortionist Tongue, Dania Ayah Alkhouli (2020)
The only thing that makes sense is to grow, Scott Ferry (2020)
Dead Letter Box, Terri Niccum (2019)
Tea and Subtitles: Selected Poems 1999-2019, Michael Miller (2019)
At the Table of the Unknown, Alexandra Umlas (2019)
The Book of Rabbits, Vince Trimboli (2019)
Everything I Write Is a Love Song to the World, David McIntire (2019)
Letters to the Leader, HanaLena Fennel (2019)
Darwin's Garden, Lee Rossi (2019)
Dark Ink: A Poetry Anthology Inspired by Horror (2018)
Drop and Dazzle, Peggy Dobreer (2018)
Junkie Wife, Alexis Rhone Fancher (2018)
The Moon, My Lover, My Mother, & the Dog, Daniel McGinn (2018)
Lullaby of Teeth: An Anthology of Southern California Poetry (2017)
Angels in Seven, Michael Miller (2016)
A Likely Story, Robbi Nester (2014)
Embers on the Stairs, Ruth Bavetta (2014)
The Green of Sunset, John Brantingham (2013)
The Savagery of Bone, Timothy Matthew Perez (2013)
The Silence of Doorways, Sharon Venezio (2013)
Cosmos: An Anthology of Southern California Poetry (2012)
Straws and Shadows, Irena Praitis (2012)
In the Lake of Your Bones, Peggy Dobreer (2012)
I Was Building Up to Something, Susan Davis (2011)
Hopeless Cases, Michael Kramer (2011)
One World, Gail Newman (2011)
What We Ache For, Eric Morago (2010)
Now and Then, Lee Mallory (2009)
Pop Art: An Anthology of Southern California Poetry (2009)
In the Heaven of Never Before, Carine Topal (2008)

A Wild Region, Kate Buckley (2008)
Carving in Bone: An Anthology of Orange County Poetry (2007)
Kindness from a Dark God, Ben Trigg (2007)
A Thin Strand of Lights, Ricki Mandeville (2006)
Sleepyhead Assassins, Mindy Nettifee (2006)
Tide Pools: An Anthology of Orange County Poetry (2006)
Lost American Nights: Lyrics & Poems, Michael Ubaldini (2006)

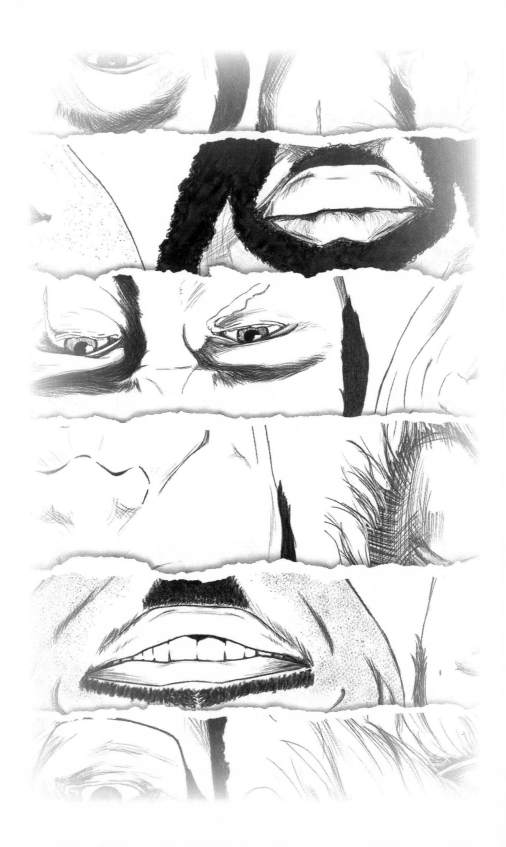

Made in the USA
Middletown, DE
03 April 2021